Price Action Trading

Day-Trading the T-Bonds off PAT

by Bill Eykyn

HARRIMAN HOUSE LTD
3A Penns Road
Petersfield
Hampshire
GU32 2EW
GREAT BRITAIN

Tel: +44 (0)1730 233870
Fax: +44 (0)1730 233880
email: enquiries@harriman-house.com
website: www.harriman-house.com

First published in Great Britain in 2003
reprinted 2007

ISBN 1-8975-9734-7
9781897597347

British Library Cataloguing in Publication Data
A CIP catalogue record for this book can be obtained from the British Library.

Printed and bound by Lightning Source

DISCLAIMER

No responsibility for loss occasioned to any person or corporate body acting or refraining to act
as a result of reading material in this book can be accepted by the Publisher, by the Author, or
by the employer of the Author. The content of the book is not to be construed by readers as
giving specific or general advice, but as an explanation of the author's personal way of trading.
No warranties are given by the Author or the Publisher as to the past, present of future
effectiveness of the methods described, or the accuracy of the information contained herein.

To Sophie

Contents

About the author

From his very first interview as a cub reporter (with Richard Dimbleby in the actual biplane used by Bleriot half a century previously), Bill Eykyn has been a journalist, writer and broadcaster. So he came to the market with a very different perspective from the norm.

He started, like so many, with a newspaper ad. This one led him to trade FTSE options on BBC2 through a broker with hot tips. After the obvious happened, he was introduced to the FTSE Futures, using a special TV aerial for the data feed. Then options on the American grain markets (via satellite and a clunking DOS program), including a hair-raising run on the Soyabeans.

Finally – and none too soon – he was introduced to the T-Bonds in Chicago by a CBOT and CME Member, where he gained a wealth of experience, in and around the pits. For several years the trading was through a satellite feed from DBC in America, but then the company metamorphosed into E-Signal and its internet feed – and these are the charts used throughout the book.

"Trading should be viewed," says Bill, "as a game played by the Big Boys, with savvy traders following in their footsteps – and this is where my concept of price action trading comes in."

This book is actually a sort of swan-song, because Bill Eykyn is retiring to a farmhouse in Andalucia, where presently there are no telephone lines. However, as soon as he can get a satellite communications system up and running, his three novels currently on the go will be put on the back burner – yet again!

Preface

What the book covers

This book is about day trading. Using the price action itself, rather than any of the usual array of indicators based on it. The US 30-year Treasury Bond Futures is the favoured instrument – the T-Bonds, as they are commonly called. There are good reasons for choosing this instrument to learn to trade – one being that they do not require a detailed knowledge of bonds themselves. The other attractions, whether you are a beginner or a seasoned veteran, are to do with liquidity, range, behaviour, patterns and the price action displayed at the key support and resistance points it encounters.

Most days the T-bonds offer trading opportunities which can be taken within a money management environment that can give you an edge for profit – and this book has been designed to show you how to do just that. Fully illustrated with charts taken from a live trading screen and displayed in exactly the way you would have seen them for yourself, on your computer monitor. What you see is not just what happened, in detail, but also clear evidence of just how you could have profited yourself from each trading situation.

Who the book is for

This book has been written for anyone wishing to day trade, using a discretionary method, rather than a mechanical system. It is a learning tool which should commend itself to the experienced trader, as much as to someone new to this business. Certainly I hope that any raw recruit would find it an easy read, even if it took a while longer to digest the subject matter as a whole.

How the book is structured

The seasoned trader will probably start by skip reading, to see if he can cut to the chase quickly. The less experienced will immediately see – from the detail of the charts alone – that there is a great deal of information to absorb, and will have to start at the beginning! After that, wherever you place yourself as a trader, I hope you will find that the methodology is pretty straightforward, the approach you need to adopt clear-cut, and the various steps involved in the process uncomplicated.

It has to be said that there is nothing amazing or wonderful in learning to read the tape – for that, albeit in a computer environment, is what this methodology is all about – and the key to success in so doing, is in the application of a robust risk/reward/ratio. This means that the successful exponent of the art-*cum*-science of discretionary trading, in this particular way, has to have a mindset that can take the winning and the losing with complete equanimity. It is not easy. It is not for everyone. But . . . those who can learn how the market works and learn to go with the flow, putting the odds on their side, stand a good chance of creating the essential edge to win.

Those who already day trade in discretionary fashion will hopefully gain pointers here and there and find, as we all know, that it often takes just one pearl gained to make the trawl an eminently worthwhile exercise. Those who come to this book with little or no experience will gain from their lack of preconception, even if it takes a lot of reading and re-reading to get up to speed on the computer, with live charts.

Glossary

To keep the narrative flowing, I have tended not to spend time explaining terms and concepts too much in the body of the text. However, there is an extensive glossary at the back of the book if you get stuck.

Supporting web site

The web site supporting this book can be found at www.harriman-house.com/pat

Best of luck

Bill Eykyn

Introduction

In exactly the same way that the chartist's work is highly visual, so too is this book. The charts, as you will see, are crowded with lines; Resistance and Support lines. They play a key role in the trading methodology and, therefore, play a key part in this book. While some are more important than others, all lines have to appear in most of the charts, if only because that is how you will actually see and use them when it comes to trading in this way.

Since most of the charts have been updated in real time, I apologise now for any typing errors or other mistakes in the text, because they are very difficult to change afterwards. Obviously, I have had to use abbreviations and they have been incorporated in the glossary. When practical, I have tried to get all the information on the chart and, where it is impossible, I have had to use the text within the page, duly referenced.

Having been brought up with the concept of a book having a beginning, a middle and an end, I have tried to explain my methodology in that way. There is an awful lot of information to absorb, but at least the subject does have a very logical sequence of events. It is important to understand this and appreciate that certain things happen, or have to be done, as a matter of routine. The markets may be random, but the humans involved in it are for the most part creatures of habit. For example, every day at about the same time the Big Boys, as I call them, leave the pits and go for their lunch - or brunch! Their return is like clockwork. You can almost set your watch by them. Knowing this is vital information, and the significance of their return and how they act can help you to make money. But you would be surprised how few traders know about this – let alone how to take advantage of it, even though it happens every single day.

To day trade successfully, it is essential to have a large, liquid market, which you can dip in and out of, without being noticed. The trouble is that such markets – like the S&P or the FTSE – are also very volatile and are renowned for their wild swings. This makes it very difficult for the smaller trader to stay alive long enough to reap the rewards. Small people simply cannot afford big stops; for them, the market has to be of temperate volatility and within a smaller average range, as well as being large and liquid.

This is precisely what the T-Bonds are all about. As you will see, the instrument is ideally suited to the smaller trader who wants to day-trade. Furthermore, the market does, in my view, move generally at a pace which can be read and confirmed, most of the time – and certainly in time to place trades in an ordered fashion.

For the day trader, working in small time frames, there is no doubt that price action is the king. It is the leading indicator. There is nothing more up-to-date, on the mark, or a better gauge of what is likely to happen next. All of the other commonly-used indicators lag the market. It is using this fact, within various different time frames, set against the resistance and support in the market, which will produce trading opportunities for the astute observer of price patterns.

Price action is the very essence of day trading and the rationale of this book. You will see exactly how to lay out your stall before the day starts and then trade in tune with the market; hopefully you will be able to see how the market can be read and traded and, if you like, through the new(ish!) concept of spread betting test out the methodology *in the market* with very little capital involved.

Establishing a home-based trading business

home office – data delivery – computers & peripherals – charting packages

The home office

Working from home may sound all very relaxed and stress free and, compared with having to commute to town for the daily toil, it probably is. However, trading from home – or anywhere else for that matter – is anything but relaxed and certainly not stress free! The advantages of being at home can be considerable, but you must not let the several disadvantages and distractions work against you.

As every seasoned trader knows, trading is a business and must be treated as such. It is, therefore, essential to turn a part of your home into a business environment and it is important to get this right, before you do anything else. So whatever facilities you have now, take this opportunity to review your situation.

Clearly, the very first thing that is needed is a room wholly devoted to trading. One in which you will feel comfortable to be in, for many hours at a time. Consider, therefore, the logistics.

The trading room

This is very much a personal matter. Since you are working from home, make it feel like home, rather than an office. In fact, think of your room as a study, because you are going to be doing a lot of that. It is handy if a bathroom and the kitchen are within easy reach. Murphy's Law dictates that you will want an in-take or out-take at precisely the time when you are in the middle of a trade.

Also, for those occasions when you are overcome and feel the need to collapse, it's good to have a decent sofa you can stretch out on, but make sure you still have a clear view of the screen. You will, of course, need a really comfortable, high back, swivel chair, from which you can feel totally in command of your work station.

The electrics

The array of equipment required to trade is startling and you will need to put some real thought into the way in which you organise it. Lighting, too, is crucial: when staring at computer screens it is important that you do not get a bad reflection from the lights on them, and you need be able to subdue the lighting when taking a rest. Another thing that you will find is the need for far more power points than you can imagine, for all the electrical gadgetry, such as:

Computers	Monitors	Printer	Telephone
Modem	Television	Control Box	Satellite Box

| Scart Box | Kettle | Fridge | Coffee Maker |
| Desk Light | Fan | Vacuum Cleaner | |

One of the consequences of all these power points is that you will have trailing leads that will need protection, especially if you have animals around the place with access to your new sanctum.

The equipment

Such is the incredible and continual advance in technology that it is impossible to recommend a particular type, let alone make, of computer/monitor/printer etc, but you must consider the basics involved. In other words, that the computer has all the processing capacity required to deal with the in-flow of data, at all times, including surges during fast markets; that the monitor is large enough to view what you want to see, within the resolution that suits you. Consider the data coming in as the life-blood of your machine and that all the lines on your charts are the arteries and veins along which it travels. While what you do with this life-force from the markets is one thing, without the speed and clarity of the information, you stand no chance of making timely trading decisions.

Data delivery

The two most common forms of receiving the essential data that you need to trade are satellite and the internet. The former is probably the most reliable, but also the more expensive. The latter is getting more reliable, but is much cheaper to install and run. With both, you need a telephone back-up system – preferably land-line and mobile.

Satellite systems

It was satellite that first brought the cost of real-time trading the American markets within the reach of ordinary people. Until then such major markets were only the province of professionals, but as soon as a satellite dish could be erected not just for domestic television viewing, the home trader was born. Now, the original providers of those systems have, themselves, moved away from satellite and are the main providers of the internet-based services.

Since the specification of the dish is not far different from the many you see on houses up and down the country, you will not find it difficult to track down a local installer. These are the basic factors which have to be taken into account:

1. As a prerequisite, check that the dish can be pointed at the satellite concerned, without any obstruction from your property. Check too that a neighbouring house, wall or tree is not in the line of sight, or in any way likely to could cause a problem.

2. Check whether planning permission from the local authority is required to put a satellite dish on your house. Every locality will have its rules and, since it is such a vital part of the business you are trying to set up, you must find out the position before you start in earnest.

3. Make sure the dish can be secured very solidly and that you are covered by insurance for any damage to your house or equipment as the result of a lightning strike. (Mine is actually on the side wall of a building, rather than the roof, and the bracket was made by our expert welding farmer friend, to a rigorous specification that would see the wall collapse before the dish!)

4. The wiring will end up in a so-called black box, which has to be tuned like a television set. If the satellite is to run a data feed service as well as a television, it will need a double node and a lead will run to a small, usually grey, box with flashing lights on the front of it. Because all the lights on the grey box are meant to be at green and, for reasons various, sometimes go red or orange, it is important that this piece of equipment is visible. There is also a panel on the front which resembles a ticker-tape with the price data from the various exchanges you have subscribed to, moving from right to left; this, too, must be visible from where you sit. It has to be situated, if not directly and distractingly in your line of sight, then at least with the face of it in such a position that it will catch your eye from time to time. Red lights generally mean you are not receiving data and it is vital that you notice this as soon as it happens – especially if you are in a trade – about which, more later.

Internet services

For several years the unreliability of the internet prevented the serious growth of data feed systems trying to harness this wonder of technology. But, as modems got better, computer hard drives got bigger, and telephone lines got more and more sophisticated, so too have the providers of data been able to develop much more reliable and speedy feeds.

There are masses of different internet service providers and they, in turn, offer many different types of service. The basic sorts that are currently available include the following:

2-hour cut off

This is the ordinary type of domestic dial-up connection, which has obvious drawbacks, but can be used quite successfully, provided you have a good telephone line that does not break up. The reference to '2-hour cut-off' simply refers to the fact that some ISPs deter heavy use on fixed price contracts by terminating a connection after a continuous 2 hours – whereupon you have to dial-up again. This is not ideal.

Continuous

This is, at the very least, what you need when you are actually trading. There are two sorts:

- Cable: if at all possible you want this internet cable 'always on' connection.
- ADSL: the BT telephone internet 'always on' service, which is an excellent alternative.

Choosing between satellite and internet data delivery

In truth, the home-based, day trading operation has to have both satellite and internet technology, if only because a satellite feed is still the only realistic way of receiving the essential CNBC television service. Day trading relies heavily on instant access to news and events and the most important reports that come out are all American. Consequently, CNBC is a mandatory aid and, in the main, that means a satellite television service.

While most of the internet data feed companies provide a news service as part of their output, none of them are as fast or as eye-catching as a mute television monitor (operated by remote control) within the eye-line of the trader.

Computers and peripherals

If all you want to do from your work station is trade, then you can manage perfectly well with one computer – and even fairly basic models are powerful enough these days; but if you want to do other things like word processing, accounts, or surfing the internet at the same time, you will probably want two machines. Each computer can act as a back-up for the other – and that's no bad thing. Personally, I have two machines networked together, so that each one can read the other. Also, I have 19" monitors, with anti-glare screens. This really is the minimum size when it comes to setting up your charts and worksheets. Having seen 21" screens, I am now envious and it is only a question of time before I upgrade.

Your workstation will also need room for a printer, possibly a scanner, a fax and telephone – ideally two, so that incoming calls do not disrupt your ability to pick up the other phone to your broker. You will need a television for CNBC and if you can so organize your workstation that the set is straight in front of you and above and beyond the monitors, you will find this useful. The reason is that you want the screen to be constantly in your eye-line, but far enough away not to distract you from the close scrutiny of your charts. The set that I have has an interface with a decoder from the satellite, which has a hand control which I operate from my workstation. The television is mainly on mute, but as soon as there is a news flash the sound can be turned up - but more on this later, too.

Chart 1.1

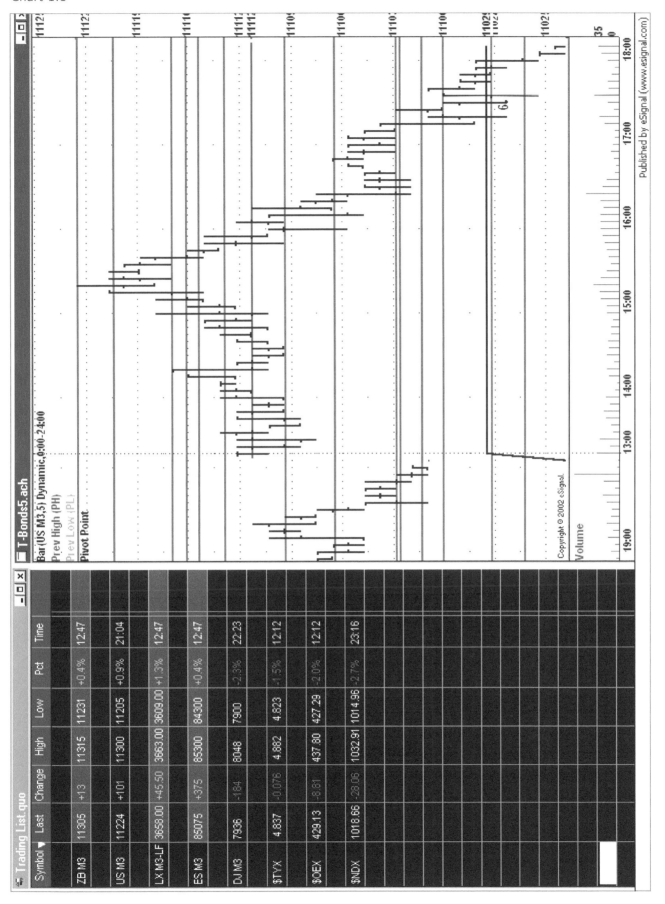

Charting packages

With the hardware sorted out, you then have to get to grips with the software. It seems to me that Bill Gates has got the market sewn up, in that you're almost bound to have Windows 98, 2000 or XP as the operating system for your computer. So any charting package is going to be Windows-based. There are quite a number of different technical analysis programs on the market and they tend to be either very basic or very sophisticated, with not a lot in between.

Before assessing the pertinent points, remember that we are talking here about charting rather than quote screens. As you can see from the chart above and analyzing the movement in real time, is completely different from having a stream of figures showing, albeit precisely the same movement, but only as a mass of changing numbers in the same boxes. You will appreciate that whereas quote screens will dominate a broker's office or bank's dealing room, because it is the actual level that the market has reached (or not!) that counts when dealing with clients' accounts, the chartist is almost wholly interested in the patterns formed by the price action, as the market moves within the different time frames, against any number of indicators and other factors represented on the screen.

Since numbers on their own mean little or nothing to the chartist, it goes without saying that quote services – whether freely provided or not – have little or no value, as a trading tool. A chartist simply cannot trade without charts and the data for those charts must arrive in an appropriate and timely fashion. And, for the small, home-based trader, one should add, in a cost-effective manner, too.

Furthermore, the chartist has to be able to read and analyze the information quickly and simply, which means that the way the chart is presented and can be manipulated is equally important. Therefore, discounting quote services completely, let us look at exactly what sort of charting package one needs to trade – and let me immediately emphasize *to day trade the type of instruments that I do*. And, thereby, hangs the major part of the tale I have to tell.

Basic charts

1. Data feed providers' own charting packages

2. Internet advertisers' charts, as displayed on the net

3. Investor services' web sites

Most of these are pretty basic, often of poor quality resolution, and with few if any indicators. They rarely permit you to change time frames or create additional charts. Having said that, one or two of the data feed providers have improved their charts greatly in recent times – as I found out to my benefit and, now, hopefully yours.

Sophisticated charts

1. General charting programs
    e.g. *Metastock*, *TradeStation* and *Updata*

2. Specialist charting programs
    e.g. *Dynamic Traders*, *Fibonacci Trader* and *AdvancedGET*

There are quite a number of other charting packages on the market, as well as programs based on specific trading concepts. The latter may run on their own or be incorporated into generic packages. Naturally, all of them will have their various bells and whistles according to their particular sales platforms. Over time, some will gain popularity while others fade, but virtually all will be based on, or include in their armoury, a host of diverse lagging indicators.

The charts I use

When *Omega Research* (now called *TradeStation*) produced a product called *SuperCharts* I was already an aficionado – via satellite. It worked in more or less exactly the same way as *TradeStation*, but it did not have a 'power editor' to write code for indicators. It could only use imported code that had been originated by others. So far as I was concerned, there were two advantages: firstly, I did not need all the indicators and other paraphernalia and, secondly, it was much cheaper.

The reason I mention this obsolete product called *SuperCharts*, is that there are still many copies floating around the market and there is a company called *Dynastore* which produces an interface which works with several of the internet data feed products – including the one I use, *E-signal*. The reason I *no longer* use this unsupported product is because I have found that the upgraded charting package which comes free with *E-signal*, combined with their excellent live support service on the internet, is perfectly adequate for my needs. Yes, it is a more clunky system than dear old *SuperCharts* but the quality of charts (seen throughout this book) is very good.

Chapter summary

When you trade, your work place, your work station and all your equipment has to function well. The software and the services have to be of the highest standard, within the parameters required to trade efficiently.

Before we get down to setting up the charts and seeing what is involved in *price action trading*, let us first look at the markets – the instruments you want to trade.

Choosing your markets

markets – range – volatility –slippage – bid/ask – T-bonds

Investing in stocks and shares has always been considered a reasonable and proper activity, but speculation in the commodities and futures markets is viewed as being only one step removed from gambling. There is clearly a certain amount of truth in this perception. But the way many people *day* trade the stock market, today, is exactly the same form of speculation as those who *day* trade the commodities and futures markets. Neither are remotely interested in the long term value of the markets. Everything hinges on what is happening today. Now. This minute.

However, those building a portfolio of shares are much akin to those position trading in say, coffee, wheat, energy or the bonds. They are interested in the longer term. The trend is important. The obvious difference is that the shares are eventually delivered to the owner, whereas unless you are actually in the business of using coffee or any other commodity, you will either roll over or liquidate your position before actual delivery of the contract. It is one thing to own some shares in Nescafe, but quite another to have a few tons of coffee beans delivered to your door!

In general terms, successful traders are those who have learned to trade and use a method or system which consistently produces profitable results. How and what they trade can be very diverse. While some will specialize in one market or group, others will spread their net over a broad spectrum of instruments. Again, there will be those who deal exclusively in options, while others will concentrate on trading shares or futures contracts. As a result, the underlying instrument might be stocks, bonds, indexes, currencies, commodities, etc. Then, on top of all that, is now the global aspect of all these markets – some of which are open more or less all the time – and accessed from many different countries, through the wonders of FM radio, cable and satellite and, preeminently these days, the internet.

Futures markets

In this book, we shall be concentrating on the futures markets, in general, and the US 30-Year Treasury Bond market, in particular. While some people will have little knowledge of the T-Bonds, they will assuredly have heard of *futures* and promptly tell you how dangerous they are. The best retort is, *So is crossing the road!* As must be obvious, when you think about it, both depend on circumstances. Try crossing a four-lane highway during the rush hour and you had better have your obituary to hand, but using a pedestrian crossing in the town centre will probably put the odds of survival on your side. The same goes for trading futures: put on a trade at the time of a scheduled economic report being announced and you will more than likely find yourself in severe trouble, but go long or short at the right time, in the right circumstances, having read the price action and you will probably survive or even succeed at making money!

Another thing you will hear, which is simply not true, is this

> *'For every winner there is a loser.'*

Paradoxically, people who quote this usually go on to say that ninety-something percent of people lose – implying, for sure, that you will be one of them. The truth is that for every contract bought, one is sold. The two sides of the equation must balance. It is a zero sum game, except for the deduction of commissions and exchange fees. The open interest within any market must have an equal number of buyers and sellers.

This is very different to saying that for every winner there is a loser. You see, a trader may be entering the market by buying $100 off a seller, who was delighted to sell because he had already made a substantial profit before he sold his holding. While the two sums are offset against each other, the seller has already made a profit, while the buyer still hopes to – but may not, when he comes to liquidate his position. It is this important, if subtle difference, which in my opinion negates the 'for every winner there is a loser' reasoning. Despite all the competitiveness in the market, the fact remains that at the moment you think you ought to enter the market is when you enter. You may or may not suffer adverse slippage and the market may or may not go the way you want it to go. When you come out (with positive or adverse slippage), you have either made a profit or a loss, or perhaps broken even. The result to you is the fact that counts and what happens next time, is next time. The market is always right and so are you sometimes – hopefully more often than not!

All one can be sure about is that there have to be many, many winners in any market or there would not be a market for very long. By the same token, there have to be a goodly number of losers, as well. That's life. All markets are made up of a mass of different people, with divergent views and expectations about what the future holds. It is important to understand that the origination of the *futures* markets was to transfer risk from users of the cash product, known as *hedgers,* to *speculators* who are willing to assume that risk in pursuit of profit.

For example, in the grain market you have the actual farmers who grow the product and manufacturers like Kellogg who produce the breakfast cereals, both seeking to hedge their future risk. This may be a hedge against over or under supply because of the weather and other factors. The speculators, who accept the other side of the hedgers' trades, do so in the hope of making a profit from assuming the risk. The same goes for coffee, cocoa, sugar and all the other commodities – including bonds.

Nowadays, the whole concept gets complicated by the fact that many hedgers are also speculators and each may have a foot in the other's camp as well.

Types of trader

Leaving aside the many facets of the market and the reasons why different parties get involved in it, let us now look at the different types of trader, and how they operate.

1. **Position trader**

    The position trader trades long term. While daily price action is a significant factor, his main consideration is the actual fundamentals of the market.

2. **Day trader**

    The day trader trades very short term. As you will see, he relies almost solely on technical analysis. His style of trading is very news driven.

There are of course traders who have a foot in each of these camps too.

Position trader

To be a successful *position trader* you must have a good fundamental knowledge of the market and you also need a high level of capitalization, because the market swings will be greater; you will also put on fewer (but often much larger) trades.

The position trader is looking for the longer term trend and, as such, has to carry over the business from day to day, week to week, with all that that entails. Because of the longer time frames involved, the position trader will often track several markets and spread his endeavours over several different instruments, to try and effect a balanced portfolio. He may well trade using a delayed feed or with end-of-day data and, depending on his approach, it may be quite feasible for him to do other things around trading – whether business or pleasure. Compared with day trading, it is, as they say, a whole different ball game!

Day trader

The day trader, on the other hand, has to grind out a profit every day, to put bread on the table. Such a person, usually using very limited resources, is trying to earn a living, rather than becoming wealthy. For a day trader it is his day job. He must learn to be proficient, because it is essential that he succeeds – or he must do something else.

Unlike the position trader, who is often speculating with surplus funds which he can allegedly afford to lose, the day trader needs to get to the point of being able to trade profitably as soon as possible – or if not, then at least attempting to do so within a budget that will not leave him destitute, should he fail. Too often, people start trading without having anywhere near the amount of knowledge they need to have to survive, let alone succeed. For most, learning this business becomes a baptism of fire, with too many people getting rather more than their fingers burnt. So, as a prime goal, let's try and make sure that you are not one of them, whether or not you are a seasoned trader in other markets.

By definition, *day trading* means just that: trading the market each day, only from the opening bell until the close. You are never in the market over night. You will never have a position in the market to keep you from your slumber. You sleep nights – and start afresh the next day! But what market(s) and why? Well, this is the bit which will, hopefully, save you a lot of anguish and heartache finding out.

Market profile criteria for day trading

So, let us first see what the basic tenets are for day trading.

A big enough market in which to get lost

It is vital to choose a market which is big enough to be able to dip in and out of at will. This means that it must be really liquid. Even during lunch-times or on quiet days, you want to trade a market that will not notice you. It is important that you feel whatever size of order you want to place, the market will be able to absorb it without trace. Even if you are putting on large multiple orders. Also, in case of accidents, you ideally want a market that trades overnight. If you have found yourself still in the market on close (rather than having exited as you thought!), you want to be able to get out, as soon as you find out, and not have to wait until the open next day.

A good daily range

Clearly you need a market with a good daily range, but not one that can kill you! A market that can open with huge gaps and have a daily range that fluctuates excessively is dangerous for the smaller player.

On the other hand you do not want such a miserable range that the market hardly moves in one direction or the other – like the Eurodollar often does. Traders want and need movement to make money, but the daily range must be in line with worst case expectations, if you get caught on the wrong side.

Sufficient volatility for action

It is a highly volatile market that can wipe a trader out faster than practically anything else. Big fast swings can do tremendous damage to any account. You will always hear the stories *from* traders who have made a ton of money on a fast market, but it is the stories *about* traders who lost fortunes in similar circumstances which are legion. You certainly need a market with some decent volatility, but it has to be the type of volatility that you stand a chance of using, rather than being wasted by.

Little or no slippage

Markets have to move up and down for anyone to make (or lose) money. There has to be sufficient volatility, allied to a decent range, for the market to be tradable. If a market just goes sideways in a tight range, off-floor traders cannot do anything. There needs to be decent intraday movement. On the other hand, if a market has too much volatility it becomes dangerous and it can cause a lot of *slippage*, which means movement of the price (usually adversely) from the point where you want the trade executed to the point where the trade is actually executed. Certain markets, like Pork Bellies for example, are very prone to a phenomenon which can cause extreme slippage and that is *limit moves* (i.e. when the market has moved the maximum amount allowed under the Exchange rules during a trading session). Those in that market, at that time, are locked in it until trading starts again – which might be a further limit move away . . . and another . . . and another. The piggies are famous for it, with small fortunes having been won and lost!

Bid/ask of a tick

You do not want a huge disparity between the bid and the ask price. For example, as many as six ticks on either side of the price of the FTSE is not uncommon; a whole large point on either side of the S&P is not uncommon either. Large spreads and unhelpful slippage are what brings day trading into disrepute with many traders. What you are looking for is nice bid/ask spread of just a tick – really, just a tick – in a market with a decent range, reasonable volatility, reasonable slippage and a reasonable trading cost per contract that can be afforded. It does exist . . .

Why the 30-year Treasury Bonds?

A huge, very liquid market, with a good range, decent volatility, low slippage and a bid/ask spread of usually just one tick, the T-Bonds measure up very well to the criteria above. More than that, the bonds are driven by reports and news, to produce a market which is excellent to read and to practice the concept of *Price Action Trading*. It is as good a market to learn on, as it is to make money on.

Whilst many will claim that trading this instrument is like watching paint dry most of the time, the truth is that what it lacks in the excitement associated with the volatility of the S&P or the FTSE, it gains from the steadiness of its measured tread, to make it a more readable market. As with other instruments, much depends on the price action as it engages support and resistance, but what is so good about the bonds is the amount of time there is to weigh properly the chart patterns in the different time frames, so as to evaluate the risk/reward of the potential trade ahead.

Whereas markets like the S&P, the FTSE and other highly-charged instruments can offer very good rewards for those skilful enough to read the price action within the turmoil of the volatility, the T-Bonds offer fairly similar rewards in less dramatic style and on a more controllable basis. Having said that, there is still the same amount of potential for getting things wrong, but hopefully with rather less hurt to the bank account. The good thing, as you will see, is that there are ways and means of testing your own particular skill at *Price Action Trading*, without the need to put up or lose hefty chunks of capital.

In the chapters ahead, you will see not only the concept of *Price Action Trading* being applied to the bonds, but also to the more volatile markets, as mentioned. If you can react at the different speed required and have the communications to deal with the logistics of entering and exiting those markets effectively, broadly the same principles apply. Personally, I choose the bonds – and long may they last, notwithstanding the Fed's decision not to issue any more for the foreseeable future. (See the appendix for the text of Treasury press release).

While the volume of the T-Bonds may have gone, it is still, by any standards, a huge amount and the instrument is still just as liquid, as it ever was. So from a trading perspective, nothing has altered.

Setting the scene

charts – looking left – yesterday's high & low – pivots – pit pivot system

Before all the trading throughout the world becomes electronic, you ought to, if you have not already done so, see one of the great open outcry pits. It is an education in itself. Just the sight of that vibrant mass of people in their colourful crumpled jackets, their excuses for a tie hanging round their necks and their universal Nike footwear, will make you realize that trading is a whole world apart from ordinary, every day living! Personally, I shall never forget actually walking through the bond pit in Chicago and viewing from the gallery above the frenzied action of the S&P pit – watching it turnover around $50 million a minute. A minute!

You soon appreciate that this is a place where young men (and very few women) live a life at the cutting edge of computer technology, while at the same time using the oldest sign language in existence to communicate with each other. I came back with a wonderful photograph, which hangs in my office, as a constant reminder of what it's all about. The picture, a writhing mass of colourful humanity set against an ever-changing background of liquid crystal lights flashing the latest prices, is entitled "*Movement*" and that does, indeed, sum up the whole atmosphere.

Whether one is talking about the runners racing to the floor with their orders, the frantic gesticulations of the locals as they vie to catch each others' attention, or the constantly moving ticker tape and banks of flickering monitors, the whole business is encapsulated in that word *movement*. Directly the bell sounds for the start of day until it rings again at the end, the whole place is just constant *movement*. The Bond pit is just a broiling sea of people, the noise thundering around the arena like crashing waves on the shore; and individual shouts and screams from the traders are like crazed gulls calling over the swirling froth of a tempest. To think that anyone dare launch their ship of fortune upon such a violent sea, is in itself amazing.

Technical indicators prove disappointing

It is perhaps only when you have seen the pits in action, that you realize that there just cannot be a Holy Grail system to beat the market. It is just not on – and even if it were, it certainly would not be among the plethora of indicators and programs for sale, that purport to show where the market is going next. Over the years I have tried many different indicators and each one, in turn, has proved more disappointing than the last. Here are few, taken at random from about 100 in my defunct *SuperCharts* Analysis Techniques Indicator Box:

Technical indicators that didn't work for me

AccumSwing	DMI	Parabolic
ADX	HurstMovAv	ROC
AIQLines	Keltner Channel	RSI
Bollinger Bands	Linear Regression Channel	Stochastic
Chaikin Oscillator	MACD	Swing Index
Comm Channel Index	McClellan Oscillator	Tick Line
Detreand RSI		Ultimate Oscillator

Perhaps, for those who trade much longer time frames – days, weeks and months – some of these indicators may help; but for the day trader glued to charts marked mainly in minutes, there really is nothing more accurate than the actual price action itself.

Most day traders accept that virtually all indicators are supremely right *after the event*, and complain loudly about the fact that they seem to have that horrid habit of ticking up or down at the very last moment, when there is no chance of being able to use the information. Simple systems, like cross over moving averages, are exactly the same. They will be correct afterwards, but simply do not have the ability to do the business beforehand. The best you can expect is confirmation or perhaps a helping hand to stay in a trade – but then the price action will do that for you anyway! The plain fact is that virtually all indicators are *lagging* and what you are really wanting is a *leading* indicator. Since a leading indicator would *de factum* be the Holy Grail, you can be sure that it isn't. The nearest you are going to get is the *price action* itself. There is nothing more accurate, nor faster, so this is what you must use. And, as you will find out, it is the way you use it that counts.

By the time you finish this book, you should be able to put into practice – with a reasonable prospect of success – a methodology that uses the *current price action* in conjunction with the history 'on the left', before trading 'on the right'. It may take a little time for that idea to sink in, but just let it percolate in your mind. Once you get to grips with how the market seems to work and just what the traders use to help them trade in the frenzy of the pit, you will start to see how – with that same information in the calm of your home office – you will be able to emulate their trading.

What the Pit Traders do

The starting point for the pit traders are Yesterday's Open, High, Low and Close. In other words, the price that the market opened at, the highest it traded at during the session, the lowest it traded at, and where precisely the market closed. These are the key numbers that are used to establish the expectation of Today's action. It is from these figures that the pit trader is able to work out, according to the formula below, where he thinks the fulcrum of the market will be.

From the High, Low and Close added together and divided by three, the average trading point, called the Pivot Point, is established. It is from this point that if the market moves north one should be a buyer and if it moves south, one should be a seller.

$$\text{The Pivot} \qquad P = (H + L + C) / 3$$

Then, in the absence of any other actual support or resistance point in the market (more about which in a minute), the pit trader has to consider how far the market is likely to travel in either direction, once it has set off. Again, a simple formula produces what becomes the first point of resistance, when heading north (R1) and the first point of support when going in the opposite direction (S1).

$$\text{1st Resistance} \qquad R1 = (2 \times P) - L$$

$$\text{1st Support} \qquad S1 = (2 \times P) - H$$

Should those points of support and resistance be breached, then the calculation for the next level produces the R2 and S2 lines, which the market has to either breach or fall back from.

$$\text{2nd Resistance} \qquad R2 = (P - S1) + R1$$

$$\text{2nd Support} \qquad S2 = P - (R1 - S1)$$

As you might expect, the trader's life is not quite as simple as that. But these arbitrary lines of resistance and support (otherwise abbreviated to *res/sup*) can not, and should not, be used in isolation and it is necessary to have a much fuller picture of what the market did yesterday, the day before, the day before that and so on, in order to know what *to expect* – or at least to know to expect a reaction if and when the market reaches these areas today. But more on that later.

Now, while what you are being appraised of here is no secret within the industry (and many charting packages have the Pit Pivot calculations incorporated as a Study to put on charts), what is not so well-known is that those who use and profit from this trading philosophy re-calculate the Pivot Point, R1, R2, S1, S2 at 11.30 CST (that is Central Standard Time, which is the time zone in which Chicago is situated). This is the time when the "Big Boys", as I call them, come back into the pit, having had their usual mid-morning break and re-calculate to bring them up-to-date with Today's price action so far. However, as you will see, it is *the actual return* of the Big Boys which has a far more significant effect on the market, than any mathematics that is done. Invariably, at around this time you will see the market either make a reversal or else display a definite continuation of the current trend. It is very often a time to take profits, stand aside or look to enter a position. Certainly, it is a time to watch the market closely and assess carefully where it is in relation to the major res/sup lines. Time and time again (just look at all the charts in this book) you can see the result of what one member of the Big Boys told me they liked to do at 11.30 was 'to come back and kick ass!"

Pit traders' stacked deck!

In the pits, traders use a stack of cards on which to place their orders. On one side all the buy orders, and on the reverse the sell orders. The card at the bottom of the pack is used as a reference, with the pivot numbers and other res/sup areas marked on it.

Chart 3.1

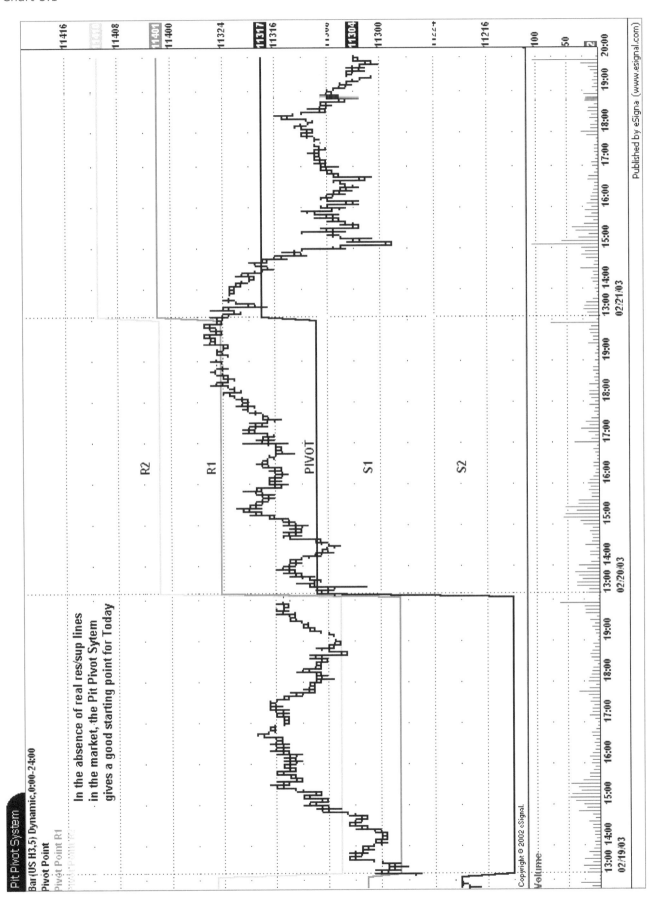

The pit pivot system, as can be seen in Chart 3.1 opposite, is a very basic concept. It is but a guide as to what might happen in the market Today, based on an arbitrary, mathematical system; as such it might be considered unreliable. However, all the traders in the pit seem to use the same formula to gauge where the res/sup is likely to come in (given that *real* res/sup areas take precedence). Whether or not it is just because the system becomes a self-fulfilling prophecy, it is pretty consistent, as guides go.

Chart 3.2

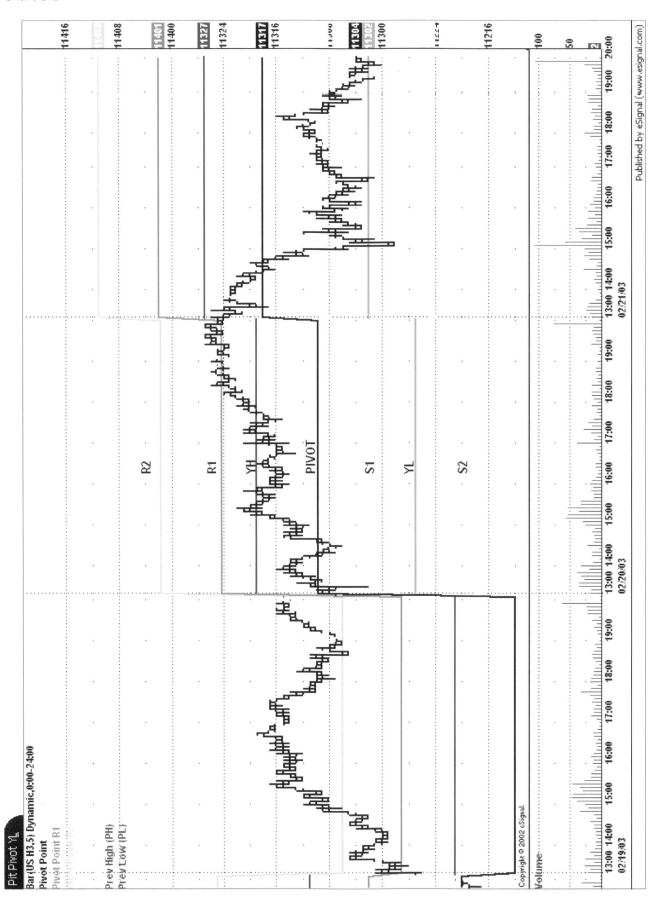

The importance of YH and YL

However, when you add Yesterday's High and Low (YH and YL), as can be seen in Chart 3.2 opposite, you can see that the market is much more prone to react to real resistance and support in the market. It is these two lines, and as they become Day Before Yesterday's High and Low (DBYH and DBYL), that are the most important for Today's action. Later you will see how other pivot points and particular key lines of res/sup come into play and, importantly, you will see exactly how to play them. However, ask most people who use res/sup lines to trade and you will often hear them say that if you only traded YH and YL in the right way, you would make money on that alone!

Chart 3.3

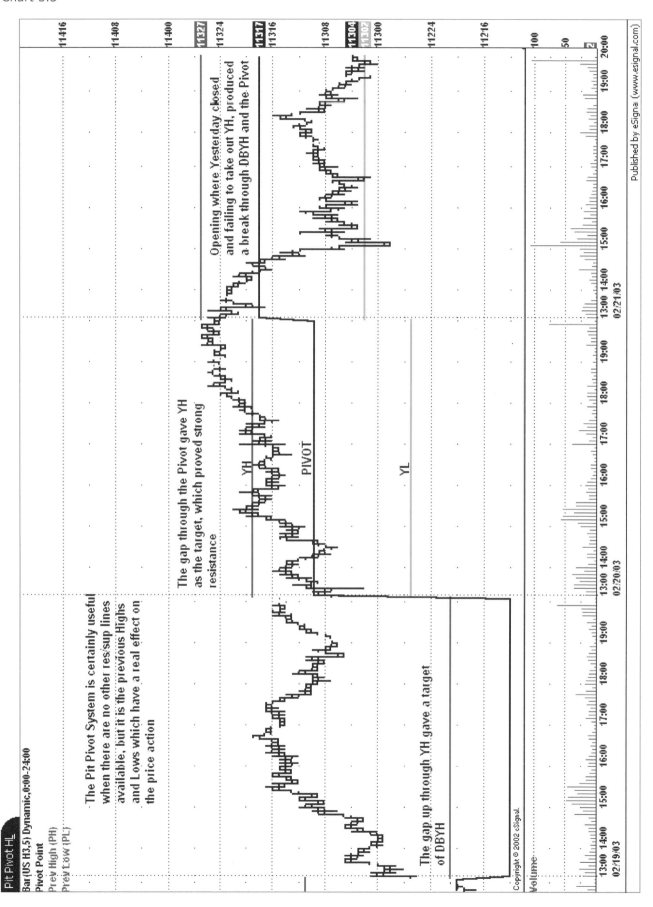

All the shouting and screaming in the pits is about the price action as it is happening there and then. A quick glance at the numbers on the back of their stack of cards, is about all the traders can do – while the off-floor traders (and the home trader!) can study charts and make their decisions in relative calm. Even then, the chartist has to have his wits about him and, as with most things, it is the preparation for the working day that can make all the difference between success and failure.

Looking left, to set the scene, before trading right

Think of the Pivot, R1, R2, S1, S2 as only the initial grid lines on your chart, from which you can see the potential for Today's action. It will not be until you have added all the other crucial sup/res lines, that you will have a real map, from which to trade. It is against one or another of these lines that the market will stall and reverse, pause and go through or else start a sideways congestion from which a breakout will occur. These are the lines that the market has to take note of and, therefore, the lines which will galvanize *you* into action!

The seasoned trader will know all about resistance and support, but if you are looking seriously at day trading using price action as the primary tool, then it is very worthwhile going over the fundamentals again and, as a result, perhaps you will look at those lines on the chart in a rather different way. First consider the sup/res areas we are talking about and then the reasons why they are so significant. After that, through many, many examples you will see that they are not a myth, a maybe, or a might, but rather that they are why the market makes it moves and gives you the opportunity to profit from the fact.

Support, as we know, comes into the market when traders think that prices have dropped to a level that make them attractive to buy. Resistance comes into the market when traders think that prices have risen to a level that make them attractive to sell. On a daily basis, such levels start at the Open, then initiate intraday Highs and the Lows and, finally, conclude with the Close. These are very significant places within the trading day. Logic will tell you that when a market opens there will be all sorts of buy and sell orders placed, as a result of the overnight action (both in the actual market itself and the effect of global activity on it). A lot of orders mean a lot of support or resistance as the market action tests or re-tests the Open – certainly during the early part of the day.

The importance of highs and lows

The Highs and Lows are without doubt the most important. If a market cannot go any higher or lower, it means that much buying and selling must have come in at those levels to support the market or resist further upward movement. As the market reaches those levels again, pressure will increase and the market will either stall and fall back or build up a head of steam and charge through. You have to know about these places – not after the event, but before, and in good time to be able to monitor the situation and react according to the price action you see unfolding in front of you.

Clearly, a Weekly High or Weekly Low is going to be significant. If for a whole week, the market has been unable to penetrate that level, there is every reason to think that there might either be a major battle between the bulls and bears or else one side is going to cave in quickly as it gets swamped by a high volume of orders. The *reasons* are numerous and academic, and as far as you are concerned, they are inconsequential because all you need to do is react appropriately. Why a market reversed off a major sup/res area or breached it is neither here nor there – at the end of the day, you either profited from it or else protected yourself against a hurtful loss. And, more importantly, the number of times you came out on top were greater than the number of times when you didn't.

Summary

So what you need to know and plot, before Today starts is:

1. The Pit Pivot calculations

2. Yesterday's High and Low

3. Weekly, Monthly, Contract Highs and Lows

4. Particular pivot highs and lows – often some time back

The way you do this on most charting packages is quite simple:

1. Create a Daily chart and 5 min chart, next to each other.

2. If your program allows, set a Study to show Previous High and Previous Low. Then using the cursor, note the highs lows on the Daily and then draw an extend line for each on the 5 min.

3. You need only do this for the bars which are within the average day's range – deleting those already on the chart from previous markings.

Look left, to set the scene, before trading right

All day traders should have that sentence on a post-it note on their screen, before they start to trade and definitely before putting on any trade. You have to keep looking left. You really do. That cannot be emphasized too much. It is always the history to the left of the chart that influences the price action to the right of the chart. The major highs and lows; the pivot highs and lows, in particular, and often the nearby res/sup points of the previous day. All these places are to the left and affect the price action to the right. Look left, before trading right. Vital!

The main chart that you will use to track the market is a five minute chart. That is about the right time-scale for you to see the overall picture, as well as the important detail. You may also be using a minute chart and a tick chart, at specific times, and also to cross-check the action, probably a 13 minute and 34 minute chart – but we will go into all that in a moment.

Just for now, study Chart 3.4 opposite and you will see how it should be marked up. By the way, the apparent clutter of lines diminishes as you get used to them and using different colours for the Pivots, for YH and YL, for the sup/res lines, and sometimes extra thickness for pivotal lines, you will not find them half so tedious. But irritating or not, these lines must be on the chart – because just look and see how the market has reacted against them.

Follow this quick tour of the day, bearing in mind that all the lines on the 5 min chart would have been there before Today started:

1. The day started by gapping down and opening just under the Pivot, but as there was a 7.30 Report (more about later) you would have waited.

2. Having closed the gap (more about later) you might have sold the turn, but the previous pivot high would have stopped you in your tracks.

3. The market turned and charged through the pivot and the line of two days before's high.

4. YH was the obvious target (more about later) for a decent trade.

5. The market then went sideways under YH, broke through nicely when the Big Boys returned – with the Pivot High once more the obvious target (again later!)

Chart 3.4

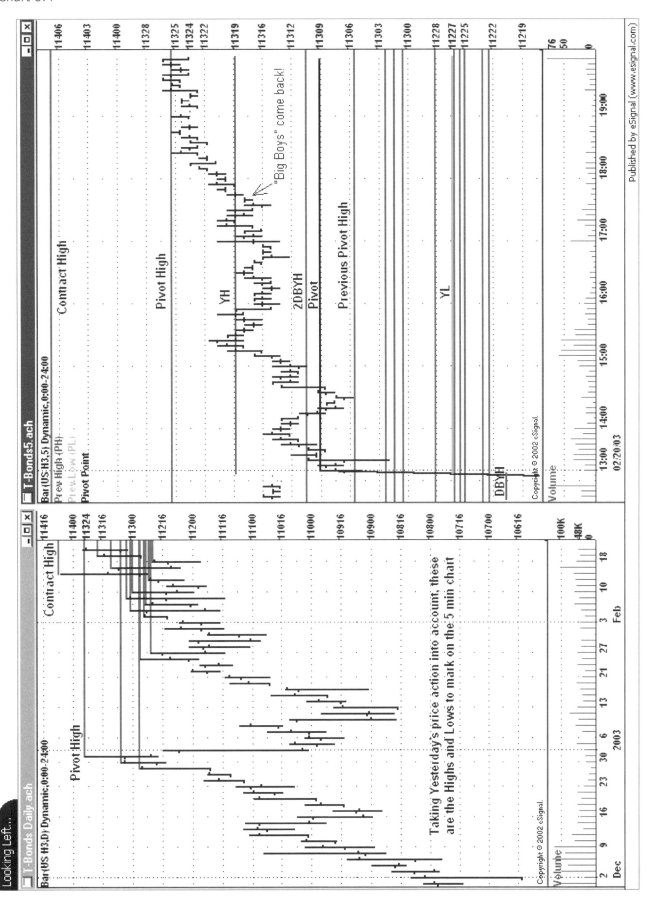

Not exactly an exciting day, but one which – without discussing a host of other factors you would taken into account – would certainly have put bread on the table. It really is vital to do your home work before the market opens. Knowing from Yesterday's price action where the market is, you can establish the likely sort of range for Today. You may well find yourself out somewhat when Today actually opens, but it does not take much to amend the chart, if most of the possibilities are already marked on it. Clearly, you need to start with as broad a picture as possible and for this you really need a daily chart which goes back several months. If you are only using *real time* data, it may only be possible to see the current contract for a month or so back – but that is probably good enough.

Unless you have continuous charts, which go back several months and years, you will probably be confined to the data from the near-by, current, month and the back month or maybe two. Somewhat naturally, day traders do not trade nights! That doesn't mean you are disinterested in what goes on when you are snoring! However, all that you need to know really, is the High and Low of the session and where it closed (which will only be a matter of minutes before it opens again). You will find that quite often the High and Low of the night session has an effect on the morning's play – but it does wear off fairly quickly.

4

Before the market opens
overnight – events calendar – Alan Greenspan & Reports – the Big Boys

The day session of the T-Bonds opens at 7:20 CST or 13:20 GMT, which means that most traders in Britain will not have to fall out of bed to sort themselves out before the opening bell. Those who trade the FTSE during the morning will want to stop and re-organize their charts for the bonds.

Setting up the charts on the screen

The way I set my charts out has evolved over time. At one stage, for example, I used to use a tick chart quite a lot, but now I find I hardly need to refer to it all. I don't want to fiddle around getting one up when I want it, so I already have it on the worksheet – but covered over by the others. A quick click on the Window button is all that is required.

Much will depend on the size of your screen and, to be frank, your eyesight. You do need to be able to read the detail and be able to see the bars ticking up and down. Better to have fewer charts visible and see them all properly, than more with less-than-efficient clarity. Some people like to have several overlapping, so that only the right edge is visible and if the whole chart is required for viewing, then a click will bring it into view – or a further click on the maximize icon and it is full screen. Personal preference and computer dexterity is the order of the day.

The main charts to have open are as follows:

1. **5 Minute Chart**
   This is full length on the right hand side of the screen and is the actual chart that I trade off, i.e. making the precise trading decisions, the order entry and exit, the monitoring of the trade, etc.

2. **13 and 34 Minute Charts** (The times to be discussed in the next chapter)
   These are on the top row of the divided screen and are used for confirming the price action on the 5 min chart. Sometimes, particularly with the 13 min chart, a formation in the making brings a greater degree of concentration on the 5 min chart, but mostly these charts are used to confirm that which you are seeing on the main trading chart is in conformity with the general movement of the market, at that particular time.

3. **Daily or 400 Minute Chart**
   This is on the top left hand corner and is mainly used for setting up the highs and lows of previous days. It is the main looking left chart to see what crucial pivot points there are, what particular large range bars might come into play, as the price action evolves. Its use much depends on where the market currently is and it is only by maximizing the chart sometimes that you are able to spot something important, from several months ago. But it is a chart that needs lots of looking at and perusing before the day begins.

4. **E-Mini or S&P 500 Chart**

For years I tracked the S&P Futures, then I decided that as I never ever would trade the instrument, I might just as well track the E-Mini (once the exchange decided to have considerably reduced exchange fees just to have this instrument alone). It is vital to have the Spoos (as the S&P is affectionately called) because of its close relationship with (what I call!) the Boos. When I first started trading the bonds they always led the Spoos, but nowadays they run in opposite directions, with the stock index futures leading. Sometimes – just sometimes! – you get a really good trade from tracking the difference.

5. **FTSE 100 Chart**

Not essential by any means, but there can be some good trades during the morning in Britain, when America is on night duty only with the Spoos and Boos. A very volatile market and mostly with ghastly spreads and fills; it is a slave to the S&P and follows its every move. Just occasionally, during its unfettered time during the morning, it will venture to move in a different direction, but it always has its collar yanked when the daytime session of the S&P starts and NYSE opens.

6. **Quote Screen**

Tucked into the left-hand bottom corner, I like to have a quote screen – mainly for the overnight action in America.

There is no need to take up extra space with charts of the overnight, but you do need to know the Highs and Lows of the bonds, as they are important numbers to mark on your 5 min *before* the open. Also, during the day it is nice to follow the Dow and the screen acts as a good check against the ticker-tape on CNBC to see how prices are moving, in relation to the feed one is getting on one's own screen.

All the charts have Volume on the bottom and you will notice the distinct blue and green lines, which mark the previous Highs and Lows, as well as the red lines for the other key lines of res/sup. The Pivot (without its attendant R1,S1.R2 and S2) is marked in black. Apart from drawing trend lines, the only other tool I need and use constantly is to mark up the Fibonacci Retracements (more about which in the next chapter).

Chart 4.1

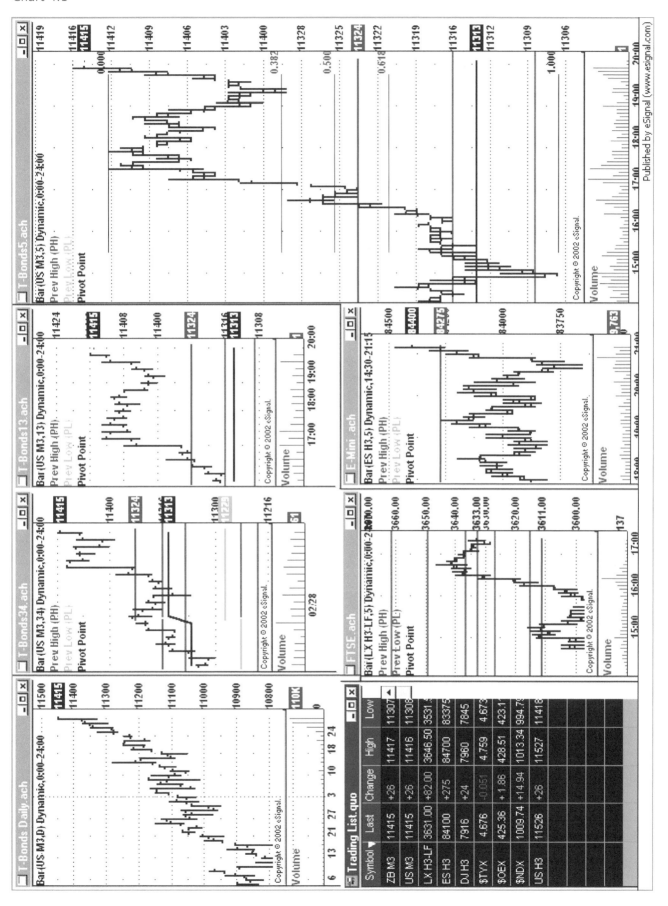

Calendar of Economic Events

With your charts done, you now have consider what events, if any, are going to effect how Today starts, progresses and concludes. While the stock indexes can be hugely affected by reports and events on the worldwide stage (therefore mainly American), the bonds rely on such events to produce a much more reasonable, even if not controllable, volatility to propel the market along. You will soon see that days when there are no reports can look very different from those that have them. In any event, you need a calendar and while there used to be a plethora of them for free on the internet, now many of them have turned into a subscription service, but a few remain and, fortunately a couple of good ones among them:

- **Yahoo! Finance** (biz.yahoo.com)
  A really good and reliable source of economic events, laid out on a weekly basis – with the ability to go backwards or forwards, by clicking the appropriate button.

- **Bondtalk.com** (www.bondtalk.com)
  This source describe themselves as "the leading provider of independent and actionable information, analysis, and insights on the bond market and the economy…" and you can see a good, clear monthly calendar.

- **The Dismal Scientist** (www.economy.com/dismal)
  A very well known site, but sadly lacking for a weekly or monthly calendar for free. You can however see a useful heading of Today's Indicator with the different nation's flags flying against any report due out by that country, Today:

- **NASDAQ** (www.nasdaq.com)
  This is the one I use most, since it is provided by E-Signal as part of their charting package and all it takes is a click to put it on the screen, as just another window, rather than a separate one garnered from the net. It shows a week at a time and you have the ability to go to any month or day in the year. It has the added advantage of telling you when the great Federal Reserve Chairman, Alan Greenspan, is talking.

Note: All the calendars use Eastern Time (ET), while virtually all the instruments being traded or tracked are on Central Standard Time (CST), so you must allow an hour's difference.

When Greenspan talks: Keep Out!

It should be a golden rule. You see, at whatever occasion he is attending, he is as likely as not to drop a little pearl for the journalistic swine gathered before him. Furthermore, such is the speed that his words travel, that the reaction in the markets can be fulsome. While the well advertised set-pieces in Washington to the Congressional Committees will have their press releases in advance – allowing those who like to gamble to guess which way the markets will move – the real message often only comes out as part of the cross-examination by the members.

The result is that when he starts at, say, 10.00 am Eastern, to read his prepared statement, the market might move down. It may then just drift on down for an hour or more. Then comes an answer to a question which includes, let us say, an indication for a change of policy – and bang, the Spoos spike up and the Boos gap down. For several minutes the markets can go wild, and you don't want to get caught in the middle of it!

Clearly a meeting of the Federal Open Market Committee (FOMC – the body that sets the interest rate, over which Alan Greenspan presides) is a crucial one for the markets; but it is well publicized and even the actual time of the announcement is pretty accurate, so there is no reason to gamble or get caught. As for the various lunches and other events where he speaks, while they may not appear to be occasions where anything important will be said, you never know... you just don't know... all you can say is, *when he is speaking, keep out.*

However, Alan Greenspan is not the only market mover. Just as important are speeches by the American Treasury Secretary and other Administration heavy weights, which tend to get reported on CNBC – which is one very good reason for making sure that you have that channel open all the time you trade. The screen in your eye line. It goes without saying that important national figures like the President addressing the nation are moments to withdraw from day trading and sit on the sidelines.

A big game for the 'Big Boys'

So as not to get too cynical about how the market works, the best thing to do is to think of the whole business as a game. A game that is controlled by the Big Boys. While you don't have to know their names (and it might be imprudent of me to mention any of them!), their very names will quickly come to mind, after you have heard them talked about – or even hear speakers from them talk on CNBC. Their sheer size and general influence will speak for themselves, as indeed their actions speak very loudly in the pit. You would not be human if you did not think that they must make an awful lot of money by manipulation of the market.

Their whole object is to make the market move. Up and down, up and down. Sideways is hard graft and unprofitable. The market does not go sideways for long! From the market makers' point of view, all the markets work in the same way: the strong hands buy from the weak hands, push the market up, take their profit, before repeating the operation on the way down – to start all over again. This happens in all the different time frames – all the time. During all the activity, the market as a whole may be moving up in bullish mode, or else being bearish and moving down – with a mass of different trends and counter trends taking place, along with periods of congestion, etc.

The only way for the small guy to make money, is to behave like a big guy, albeit in a small way! Recognize how the game is played and play accordingly. So when one says, "Keep out of the market when Greenspan is talking" it is because you do not want to gamble at the mercy of the Big Boys, but wait and see what they do and then join the fun – on their side!

You see, it really doesn't matter what is said in a speech or what a scheduled report states, the market makers will move the market in the direction they want it to go. The talking heads on CNBC will all have differing views and they will all claim to be right, whatever the market does. Listening to their justifications can be quite hilarious, if the whole business wasn't serious – or at least the outcome was. It is the 7.30 am CST and the 9.00 am CST Reports which keep the market moving, keep the wheels oiled; they are the opportunity for the Big Boys to do what they want to do. And very often, what they want to do is to take the stops out in one direction before making the market take off in another. The great game is to lull the punters into a false sense of direction and then take the market to where they want to go. As one leading member of both the CBOT and CME told me, "We call the game Taking Money from the Public!" That sums up the whole business very nicely. Very nicely indeed.

As long as you accept that and realize that you are never going to beat the Big Boys, the sooner you will learn to follow what they are doing and try and get on their band wagon. Naturally, you cannot expect to be able to follow their every move, know what is coming next, always be doing the right thing at the right time, but you can – with the tools available and using them in a disciplined manner – be able to read much of what the price action is saying and profit from that knowledge.

Retracements and The Fibonacci legacy

Fibonacci of Pisa – .382, .500, .618 retracements

Through the combination of the Pivot System, Yesterday's Highs and Lows, as well as Looking Left for major res/sup lines, you have your map of Today, all ready to trade. You have, as it were, the hills and valleys of the resistance and support, set amongst the grid lines of where you expect the market to move. Your map is sized and sectioned so that you can see clearly the expected range of where the market will move, in different time frames. You are as prepared as you possibly can be.

However, you are not the driving force of this journey, as it is the market, itself, which is going to be responsible for all the moves. What you cannot know (nor anyone else for that matter!), is in what direction the market will go, where it will make its turns, how far it will go and how long it will take to get there. You can have some good guesses, based on the over night activity, for example, or the way the daily chart has set up or whether some long term trend line has been breached. Heaven forbid, you take note of what Mark Haines or some talking head has to say on CNBC!.

No, the answer very simply is that you have a good road map for Today, well marked up with all that you can reasonably know about the terrain you face. All that you need now is a compass and a decent pair of dividers to mark your progress and make sensible predictions about what might happen in certain circumstances. The compass you need for trading is not, of course, magnetic, but as you will see, it will in its own fashion be as good a guide to navigation, as you are ever likely to find. Because it will play such a major part in your trading life, it is essential that you have a good working knowledge of this unique tool.

History lesson

Short history lesson: a thirteenth century mathematician called Fibonacci da Pisa, who lived in that famous Italian city at around the time the Leaning Tower was built, discovered a unique mathematical summation series. (Actually, because the whole concept was used some 4,000 years earlier when the Great Pyramid of Giza was built, it would be truer to say re-discovered it.) Anyway, Leonardo Fibonacci in one of the books he wrote came up with a sequence of numbers as follows:

| 1 | 1 | 2 | 3 | 5 | 8 | 13 | 21 | 34 | 55 | 89 | 144 | 233 | 377 | 610 |

and so on to infinity.

These numbers, as you can see, are arrived at by adding the first number to the next number, having started at one. So, what is particularly interesting in that, you might ask? Well, in the process of time you will discover that individual Fibonacci numbers come into their own when applied to certain aspects of market timing; however, the truly incredible fact is that (after the first ten or so numbers) if any number in the series is divided by the number following (e.g. 89 divided by 144) the result is always .618 (to three decimal places). It follows that (after the first few numbers in the series), if any number is divided into the next lower number (e.g. 144 divided by 89) the result is always 1.618 (to 3d.p.).

In mathematics this ratio is known by the Greek letter *phi* and is called the *Golden Mean*. The principle ratios of the Fibonacci summation series (and particularly those used in the markets) are:

1.618, 1.00 and .618

From these ratios, three important percentage values are derived.

Fibonacci percentage values	
0.382	the result of the division of 0.618 by 1.618
0.500	the transformed ratio of 1.000, and
0.618	the result of the direct ratio 1.000 divided by 1.618

It is these three figures, .382, .500 and .618 that will play a vital role in your day trading. They really are the key factors. They will become the make or break. The difference between success and failure. But before we see why they are so relevant, it is necessary to have some more history concerning the manner in which the markets move.

Ask most outsiders about how the markets work and the sum of the answers you will get will add up to the word *random*. But for those on the inside, a certain chap called Ralph Nelson Elliott changed all that, and a great deal of technical analysis is now done based on and according to the *Elliott Wave Principle*.

Elliot Wave Principle

Elliott Wave is based on a notion that the markets move in waves and that these waves form repetitive patterns. It is all very clever stuff and once you understand the rudiments, you can look back on practically any chart and identify a 5-wave structure followed by a 3-wave structure and so on. Notwithstanding the fact that it is always a great deal easier to see what the market *has done*, than it is seeing what it is *going to do*, some people feel that as a result of the wave principle, they can actually forecast the market. The problem (at least for me) is that the waves may recur in market price data, but since they are not repetitive in time or amplitude, I cannot see any forecasting value in the short term – well, certainly not anything that I would put my money on.

Anyway, whatever I might say about the subject, there are masses of books you can read to absorb and come to your own conclusions. The very interesting and fascinating thing to me is the fact that the whole of Elliott's thinking turns out to be based on Fibonacci. You see, Elliott came to the conclusion that the market has *impulsive* moves followed by *corrective* moves and that –

The largest wave:	1 impulse + 1 correction	= 2 cycle
The largest subdivision:	5 impulse + 3 correction	= 8 cycle
The next subdivision:	21 impulse + 13 correction	= 34 cycle
The next subdivision:	89 impulse + 55 correction	= 144 cycle

Now, just look at all those numbers: 1, 1, 2, 3, 5, 8, 13, 21, 34, 55, 89 and 144

There is no doubt that Elliott was brilliant in his deduction that the market moves in waves. It is also quite incredible that he should come up with a whole series of patterns, all of which are Fibonacci numbers. However, there is a huge difference in spotting that the market moves in waves and being able to use this information to forecast the market. As I have said before, it is not knowing the timing and the amplitude that defeats the object in the short term – and that the concept, when applied to longer time frames, does demand a certain size of bank account to withstand the draw-downs associated with the waves not only taking their time to form, but doing so with sufficient force, at the right moment, in the expected direction, for the market to move profitably for you!

Back to Fibonacci...

For me, the *Elliott Wave Principle* is a fascinating concept to appreciate with hindsight, but far too frustrating to use with foresight. Anyway, it is the numbers and not the waves which are of interest to us – particularly the ratios .382, .500 and .618, as these are the vital levels when it comes to the market's intraday movements. In maths, the ratio .618 (or 1.618) is not only arrived at with Fibonacci numbers, but if you take any two numbers at random and add them together and progress the series in exactly the same fashion, after about ten sums the ratio will become .618. In other words, this Golden Mean or Golden Ratio is a pretty special number.

Furthermore, a derivative of it, the logarithmic spiral, is also unique, in that it has no boundaries and is a constant shape. In fact, so clever is the design of this spiral, that it can be traversed infinitely in either outward or inward direction – with neither the centre ever being reached, nor the outer limits found. Deep stuff. Rather like the psyche of the markets. But, as a seasoned trader you will know, yours is not to reason why...

All that matters in trading is to understand what has to be done, not why it has to be done! This is not easy to do, which is why there are so many people out there with tools, gadgets and gizmos to 'help' you (after the event) and tell you why the market made this move or that. The fact remains that **all you want to know is: what is the market likely to do and whether or not there is a trade for you to take.**

Well, we know that no one is going to tell you what the market is going to do (we *know* there is no Holy Grail), but what you can know is what you are going to do in any given set of circumstances and that, if you react properly each time, there is a reasonable chance of putting the odds in your favour. But, when it comes to dealing with a pit full of people, there can be little doubt that the larger, the more liquid the market, the greater chance there is of the same thing happening time and time again, in more or less exactly the same way. Measuring the strength of the market's action and re-action, as it moves across the chart, is what you have to do, so that you can take advantage of the situation.

Turn the page for a discussion of the primary trading tool you will be using.

Support/Resistance tool

This is *the* tool that you will be using for your daily act of trading. Like all the best things in trading, it is very, very simple to use. I call it the *Fibonacci Tool*, because those are the numbers that count and in my E-Signal charting package, it is referred to simply as the *Fib Retracement*.

The screen picture opposite shows, on the left hand side, an up move and, on the right hand side, a down move. The Fibonacci tool is used by pressing the small pointer on the high or low of the day and drawing the pointer up or down the page to the bar from which the market has started to come off. The act of doing this will bring up the five lines you see – expanding and contracting with your movement, up or down and across the chart. The five lines are constant in relation to each other, all the time.

A .382 retracement in an up move is considered very bullish (and very bearish in a down move). A .500 retracement is also considered bullish, but clearly not so strong. A retracement of .618 would put you on guard that the move may well not go any higher than the level from which it retraced. If the .618 is breached (and the market closes beyond this number), then you should consider that the original move has failed.

Chart 5.1

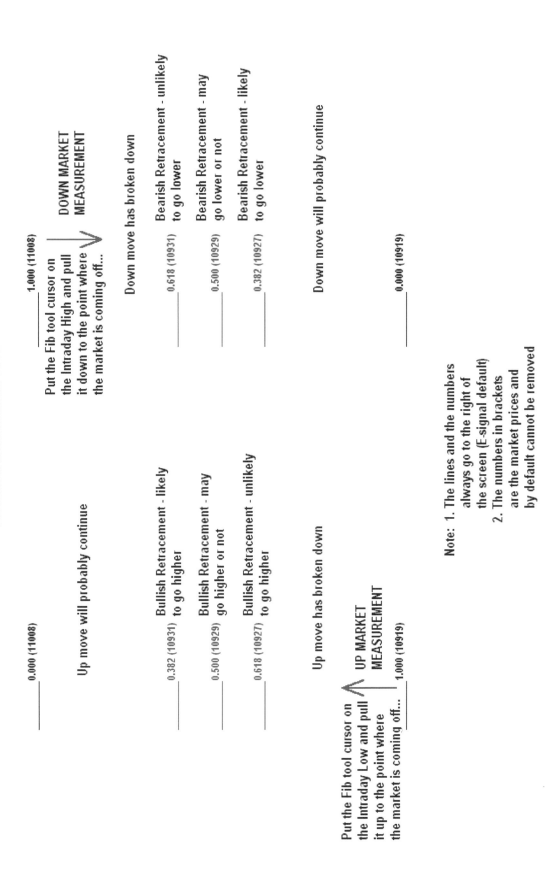

Published by eSignal (www.esignal.com)

Chart 5.2

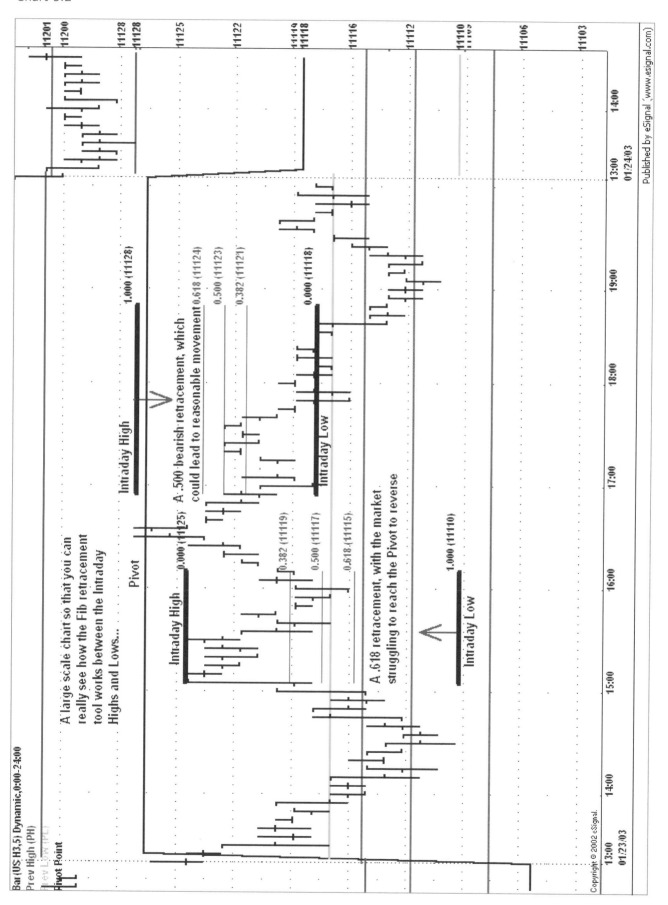

In the example opposite and on page 37 you will notice that the market went beyond the line, but the bar did not close there. It quite often does that and, thinking in terms of the game the market makers play, one should think of it as purely a 'stop taking' movement, before the market resumes its trend.

You need to study the next chart opposite carefully and when you do you will see that there is a great deal of market information there. Most of which is timely and could have been used to advantage, at the time of the price action – set in five minute bars. The particularly significant points are numbered and should be viewed with this commentary:

1. There was a 7.30 Producer Price Index Report, which your calendar would have alerted you to – following which the market retraced. The amount of the retracement is not shown to avoid too many lines at this stage, but you would have measured it and found it to be .618 and while you might have gone long through the Pivot, you would not have expected the market to go much higher – and in any case you also knew that the 9.00 Leading Indicators Report would be out very shortly, for which you would have to withdraw

2. In the event, the market pushed through YH, but stalled and started to come back or even reverse. You would immediately have put up your Fib Retracement and watched carefully.

3. The method of trading this sort of situation we will be discussing later, but suffice it to say that it was not a reversal and the retracement was a bullish one.

4. Having established that it was a bullish retracement, you would be Looking Left to see what target you could find. If you didn't join the move until the Big Boys got back, you have every reason then to go long – with good res/sup lines for your stop.

And now for the next day, which opened with a 7.30 Report (Consumer Price Index). After the usual stop taking moves (which the Big Boys often take, knowing that many traders will have stops 'behind the line' or trailing stops), the market headed south, putting up a nice wedge on YH, to get short…

5. The good fast run down ended dissecting YL with two large reversal bars and then headed north. At this point you would have put up the Fib Retracement, to measure at point 6 as soon as the market started to retrace back. This retracement is not shown (to save confusion) but it is exactly .618 and so you would not expect the market to go much further up.

6. As the market went back to point 6 when it came off again, it rather proved the point about it not going far.

7. However, the subsequent 2-bar reversal on YL seemed definite enough and perhaps this time the market would take off. Furthermore, when the Big Boys came back a 11.30 CST, they seemed happy enough with the move…

8. But . . . at point 8 we see two big up and down bars and the measurement from the Intraday Low shows .618 – so the whole move could just be a heavy retracement from the Intraday Low.

The tell-tale gap would have helped with the decision for a trade back to YL and the session's end. But at this stage we are simply looking at the retracements and we will discuss the trading of them, when you have seen more examples. It is always a burning question of whether a reversal is a retracement or not and it is often necessary to measure both ways round – i.e. from the Intraday High as well as the Low, to monitor the progress properly. In this case, it was crucial, but at least with a 5-minute chart you have a good deal of time on your side, which is helpful.

Chart 5.3

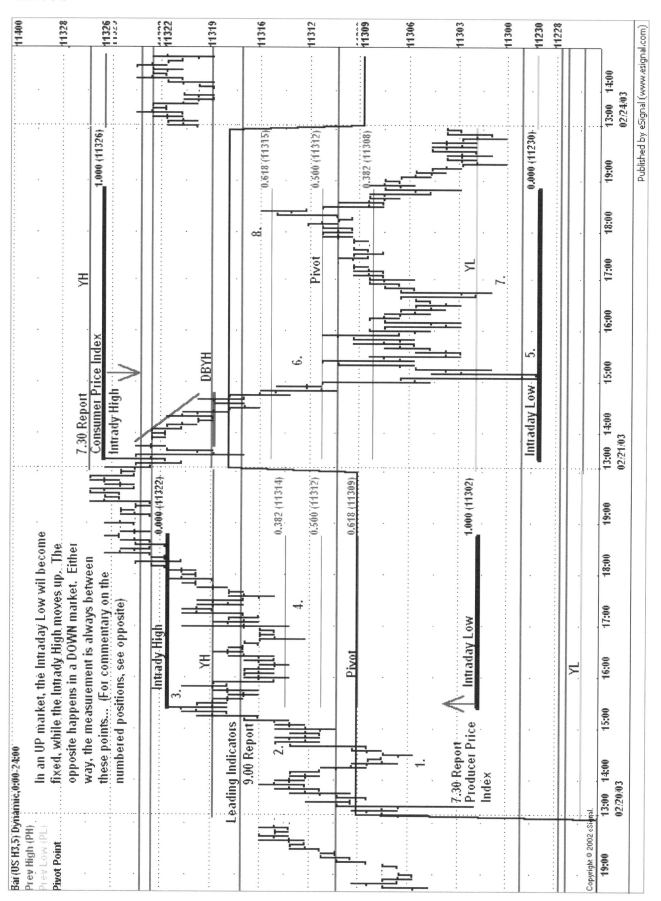

As soon as you put up the Fibonacci tool you are able to see and monitor the strength or weakness of a retracement. In fact, you have, usually, quite a number of bars of time to 'look left' and see if there are any other res/sup factors to take into account. While a retracement is an excellent opportunity and far the safest way to join a trend, what you have to be aware of is the retracement which turns into a reversal! You constantly have to be ready to cover your position when you get it wrong and, immediately that happens, try and turn your corrective action to your advantage. This is where the Fibonacci numbers and the tool is such a boon for you.

The cynical may, by now, be wondering about the wisdom of putting one's faith in a set of numbers scribbled by someone on the back on an envelope several hundred years ago. So let me add a few further facts. While the Golden Mean can be arrived at by any summation series – after the first ten or so additions – where Fibonacci has a unique quality is that all the numbers concerned play a huge part in nature and all that surrounds us, including the stars in the heavens! If you want to investigate thoroughly, just put the word Fibonacci into a search engine on the internet and see what you get. You'll be astounded. Let me give you three examples:

1. Fibonacci's Rabbits

800 years ago he pondered a question of how fast rabbits could breed in ideal circumstances. On the basis that rabbits can mate after the first month, if you start with one pair and let nature takes its course (and presume that none of them die and that the female always produce a new pair!), then from the second month on, what would the progression be? Answer as follows and note the numbers in the far column.

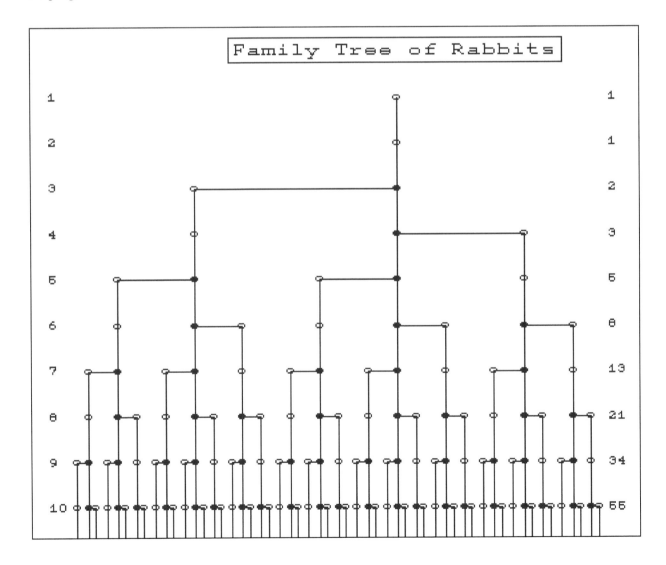

2. Trees and Leaves

The way the palms leaves grow on the trunk of the tree appear to be in spiral sequences of 5,8,13, and 21. Fibonacci helices can be seen on pine-cones, pineapples, thistles, teazles and heads of sunflowers and the like. It is common for leaf arrangements to be in similar sequences and in the daisy family formations of 13, 21, 34, 55 or 89 petals are quite common. The sneezewort plant grows both its branches and leaves in a Fibonacci sequence, as below:

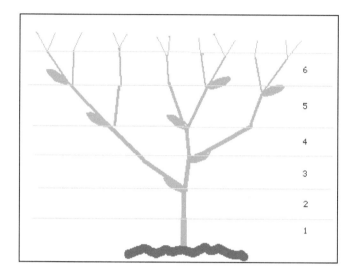 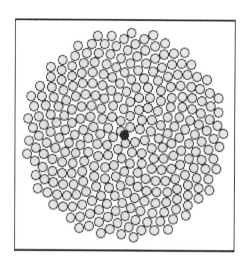

3. Fibonacci Spirals

If you put together quarter circles – each based on a new square of sequential Fibonacci numbers – so that each new square has a side which is as long as the sum of the latest two square sides, you will create a spiral. An exactly similar curve like this occurs in nature in the shape of a snail or sea shell – and it will hardly surprise you to learn that the rectangles of the spiral increase in size by a factor of 1.618... It would also appear that all the spirals in the heavens and galaxies above are formed in similar fashion.

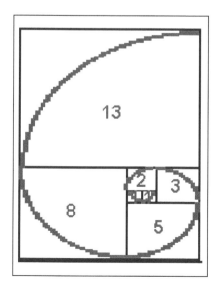 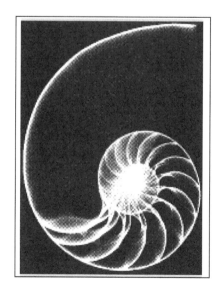

Amazing stuff, isn't it? Consequently, it seems to be more than just an act of faith to use time frames that tie in with the same numeric system as the ups and downs of life, nature and the markets!

So now you know why I use a 13 rather than a 15 minute chart, a 34 rather than 30 and – usually hidden away behind – a 55 rather than an hour chart. Apart from being fascinated with the way all the Fibonacci numbers impact on our world, I think working in very slightly different time frames from, as one might say, the common herd, means that rather fewer people are seeing and acting on what I am seeing than would otherwise be the case.

In fact, such is the importance of the Fibonacci tool and the retracements it measures for you that you really do have to *believe* that the actual figures of .382, .500 and .618 work many more times than they fail. Furthermore, you also have to *believe* that as the market is doing its retracement, you are, a lot of the time, going to make the correct decision based on the information available to you *before* you have to decide on whether or not to take the trade. Everyone can be wise after the event, but the whole purpose of this exercise is to show you that there is every opportunity with the less volatile moving T-Bonds, of being wise *before* the event.

That is not to say, by any stretch of the imagination, that you are going to be right all the time. What it does mean, is that, with good money management (which we will come to later on), you can develop a method of trading which will allow you to make enough correct decisions to get the crucial edge you need to be successful. Therefore, what you need to see, here and now, through this book are more than enough working examples of the Fibonacci tool's marvellous track record in showing what the market is likely to do. Having said that, you must bear in mind all the other res/sup issues that have to be considered, because in trading nothing can be taken in isolation.

Anyway, look at another example, before we consider the important subject of pattern recognition, as a crucial part of price action trading.

Chart 5.4

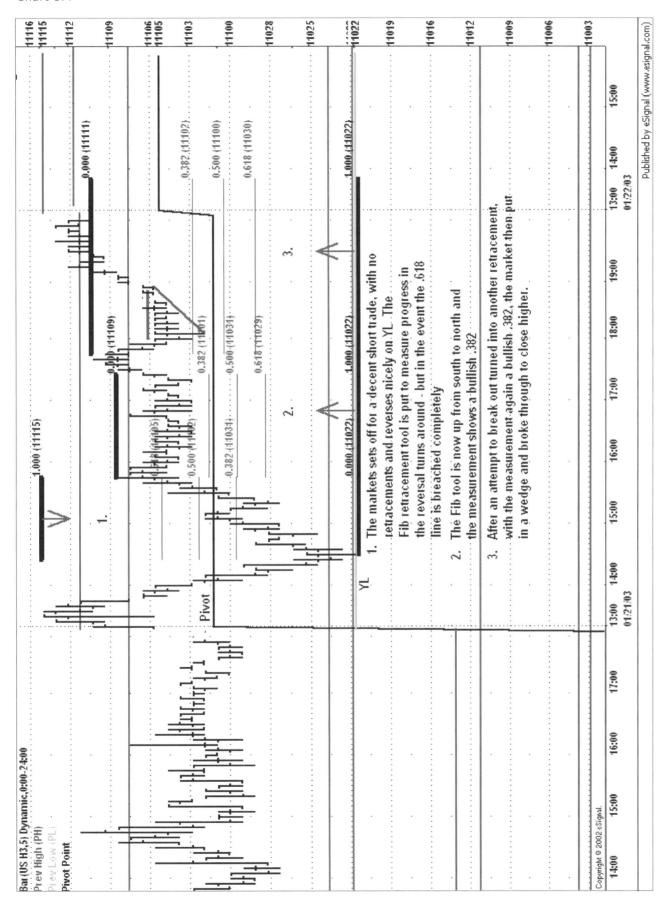

1. The markets sets off for a decent short trade, with no retracements and reverses nicely on YL. The Fib retracement tool is put to measure progress in the reversal turns around - but in the event the .618 line is breached completely

2. The Fib tool is now up from south to north and the measurement shows a bullish .382

3. After an attempt to break out turned into another retracement, with the measurement again a bullish .382, the market then put in a wedge and broke through to close higher.

Published by eSignal (www.esignal.com)

Pattern recognition and price action

price patterns - volume - reversals - breakouts

To put the vital subject of pattern recognition into context, it would be sensible to sum up where we have got to so far. Through the Pivot system and 'Looking Left' we have the basic grid lines of our map for Today, as well as all the main hills and valleys of resistance and support marked on it. This gives us a pretty good idea of the landscape we have to negotiate. Then, when we bring the Fibonacci compass to bear on the price action, we are able to see how strong or otherwise a move is and whether a retracement is a retracement or a reversal. In other words we have a well-marked map and we now want to read the road signs. We need to know the equivalent warning of the double bend, the T-junction, the slippery road, motorway ahead, etc. We must know the signs and these take the shape of price patterns.

As a seasoned trader, you will be well used to seeing the common patterns, such as a *double top*, *head and shoulders*, *upthrust* and so on (and you will certainly see these in the examples we will be looking at) but what I want you to see is the way certain patterns, when they appear in particular circumstances, produce actual trading opportunities. These occasions, of course, have to be assessed in terms of a risk/reward strategy, with sufficient time for you to evaluate a trade, make an informed judgment and then implement your decision.

The market, as you know, will do one of two things: it will either be trending (up or down) or else going sideways (in congestion of some sort). Much, of course, depends on what time frame you are looking at. For example, the market may be in an overall up-trend on a daily basis, but in a down-trend on an intraday basis, while yet again, going sideways when viewed on a five minute chart – for the last hour! Sticking with our simile, you may find yourself going up a hill, but just on the start of a short decline, having initially gone a dozen steps on a piece of flat ground. Regardless of the length of the road on the map, what you want to know is where you are at that precise moment and what's in store at the next corner and does that bridge over the stream look okay or could that scree on the hillside suddenly descend on you and what are the odds that… You've got the picture, I'm sure!

Let's start with some of the basic price patterns (illustrated in Figure on page [   ]) that are constantly seen on the T-Bonds and other instruments. It is by no means a comprehensive list, nor does it include various broad price formations and movements that will be covered in the next chapter. Further examples will also be seen in the chapter on trading strategies.

1. **Upthrust**

    A large up-bar that – give or take a tick – is a Doji, starting and finishing on the lows. Often referred to as a Telegraph Pole for obvious reasons, it is a particularly spectacular single-bar reversal when seen in new territory.

2. **Downthrust**

    Simply the reverse of 1. but somehow it often has a larger tail, when seeking out the stops before reversing the market.

3. **2-Bar Reversal**

Much more common than the first two and very often the big bar reversals tend to head off directly, which can lead to bad fills or no trade at all. As usual with all patterns, everything depends on where they are seen and at what time.

4. **Picking Up Stragglers**

That is the name I gave to this pattern, in that it is really just small retracement which allows you to get on board, when you had either missed the boat and was left as a straggler on the quayside, or were just feeling dubious about the signal. I always think of it as the Big Boys taking out the trailing stops (which they know will be there, in the market!) before getting on with the move, they had decided on.

5. **The J-Hook**

Another spectacular reversal, often seen deep into new territory and one feels it is designed by the Big Boys to get all the bulls who have been nervous about accepting their invitation to join the ball, to do so – before, that is, they announce the last waltz!

6. **Reverse J-Hook**

Mirror image of the same animal and, while not illustrated, this exceptionally good pattern is seen in as many instances for reversing south, as north. If you are lucky and the move closes on the res/sup bar you need for your stop and there is a small entry bar for your trade, you will often get a really good move following a J-Hook.

7. **Tell-Tale Gap**

In this instance, seen following the J-Hook, it is that little gap that so often appears as the market is about to race away. With a fast reversal, you ought to be in the trade and just use the gap as a confirming tool – or perhaps to add, if in the mood! It is a good signal on the bonds, because they normally move with such a measured tread, that it is nice to see them look as if they are going to break into a trot.

8. **Classic Double Bottom (DB)**

Oft seen in all markets and, once again, it depends very much on where and when it occurs. Cutting a solid res/sup line is favourite and a slow move away, to allow you to put on the trade. Then it is nice to see the bar thin out – especially if you get a tell-tale gap. With a move like the one illustrated, you could be sure you would be getting your Fibonacci tool out pretty shortly…

9. **Wedges: Lovely little wedges!**

A marvellous indicator of a build up of a move to come. This example shows two flat bottomed wedges. Easy to have missed the first one, but not the second one. Picking Up Stragglers would have helped a lot for the second. Again, feasibility and entry would depend on the res/sup situation and other factors. But the sign of what the market is going to do, is unmistakable.

10. **Doji Sandwich (DS)**

This is another of my names, because it is such an obvious pattern – both to see and to christen! Study these five examples[what 5 examples?] and you will see that the top one is the classic: an up-bar followed by a complete Doji – starting where the up-bar closed and the down bar starting where the Doji closed. Usually, this pattern is slightly out (and an even have a double doji in the middle), but whether heralding an up or a down move, it is quite unmistakable. You will see it again and again in the trading examples following. Once again, it is very much a question of where it is seen and when.

Chart 6.1

Price Patterns

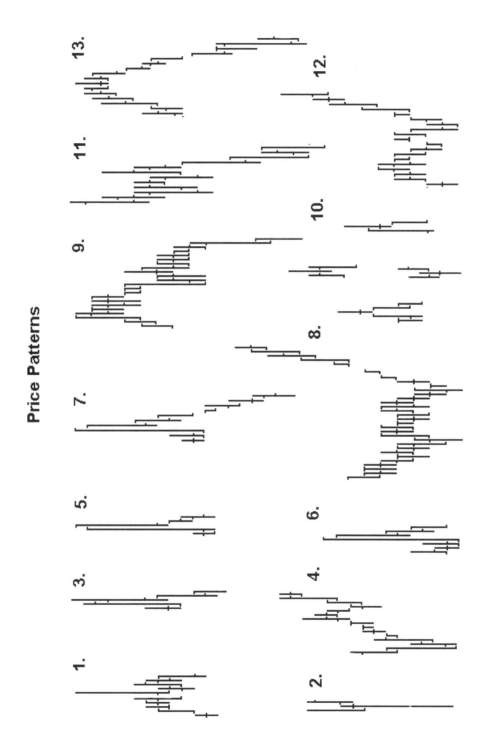

11. Third Time Through (TTT)

This is really a range (often very small) breakout pattern. In this example, the market came down to settle in a range and it could have done a TTT to the north, but in fact went south. Interestingly, if the third bar comes up to the line of the range but does not go through, then often a 'failed' TTT is as powerful the other side – but (depending very much on where it is) you can get a very good fill for the 'other side' break.

12. Another TTT

This is showing an up break, where it 'failed' on the downside and went north and through. After the failure was the time to get long (depending on where the res/sup was and what your calculation was to target). To take the trade you have to take an holistic view, but you could see the opportunity brewing and there would have been the opportunity to do something about it – if the judgment was that it was worth the candle!

13. Rounded Top (or Bottom)

This is a pattern that will grow on you, because at first you may have some difficulty in actually spotting the 'roundness' and may need to look to the more slow moving 13 or 34 minute charts to see it properly. While often having a doji or spike high in the centre, it is usually a convincing turning point in the market. This example shows a follow through tell-tale gap, with a good move ensuing – but, once again, you could expect to get the Fib retracement tool out pretty shortly.

The significance of these patterns must be assessed against a backcloth of the price action at that time. The whereabouts of the res/sup lines will prove crucial in weighing up the possibility of making a trade, let alone getting an acceptable fill against a target with a predetermined risk/reward ratio.

Most of the price patterns we will focus on can happen at any time and, it must be emphasized – if need be, over and over again – that each of the patterns have to be seen at support or resistance levels for them to be properly valid – and even then, they can turn out false. The market makers are no fools and if they can wrong foot everyone, that is exactly what they love to do. Having said that, you will find that much depends on the time frame and the particular type of pattern presented, because even the market makers have great difficulty in disguising certain moves.

The Great Game

Basically, when the market reaches a strong line of support or resistance, it has to make its mind up. You can almost hear the market makers chewing the cud. Do we break through and go on or do we reverse and go the other way? Or, shall we sit there for a while and make our minds up slowly? There again, we could fool everyone by pretending to go on up, but actually reverse – after we have sucked everyone in! It is all a great game – and they make money at it – but it is also a game you can play and also make money at, too.

You see, what the market makers do is very simple. They buy low, take the market up and then off-load their inventory. Having done that they then short sell the market, bring it down and off-load their inventory again, before repeating the cycle. Now, this is done on all time frames and while on some occasions it is very obvious, on others not so obvious. Either way, it is a very skilful operation and they use every trick in the book to fool people. They are the large players and, repeating what was said to me in Chicago, the name of the game is called, "Taking money from the public!" So, while you and I are members of the *public*, we have to act, behave and generally follow what the *market makers* are doing. They influence the market with their size and very often their footprints can be clearly seen, so what the small guy can do is put his feet in their prints and follow. We can use the same map and now must learn to read signs – the price patterns.

Identifying patterns in real-time charts

So let's look at some examples of real time charts, which have one or a number of the patterns above. They have all been marked up and annotated on screen, which once captured is very difficult to edit. A publisher's nightmare, I'm afraid, but for those who want to get to grips with day trading, I hope will be worth the study – through the maze of res/sup lines, which are vital and something you simply have to get used to – whatever charting package you use. Let me put it this way, where there are blanks (which is where I have tried to put the notes) and there are no res/sup lines it is just as vital information, when reviewing the chart. Most books opt for clean looking pages which are very easy to read, but do they have all the information you need on them? I have tried to make sure – as cleanly as possible – that the essential information is there. Where there is simply not enough room, I have had to use numbers to refer you elsewhere for the text. One last thing before we start: please see the Glossary for all the abbreviations that are used.

Example: 2-Bar Reversal and Wedge

The trade up from the res/sup at YL was not heralded by a clear cut pattern, the obvious target would have been YH, where the market reversed very clearly with a *2-bar reversal*. The market would have moved too fast for most to have got filled, but the retracement put in an angle which had the hallmarks for turning into a wedge on YL – as indeed it did! The trade down would have been good, but it was a pity that the little TTT the heavy res/sup line was halted by the return of the Big Boys. What might have been a decent *Thank You* trade also ended in a range. Two clear patterns for certainly one good trade – and no losses.

Chart 6.2

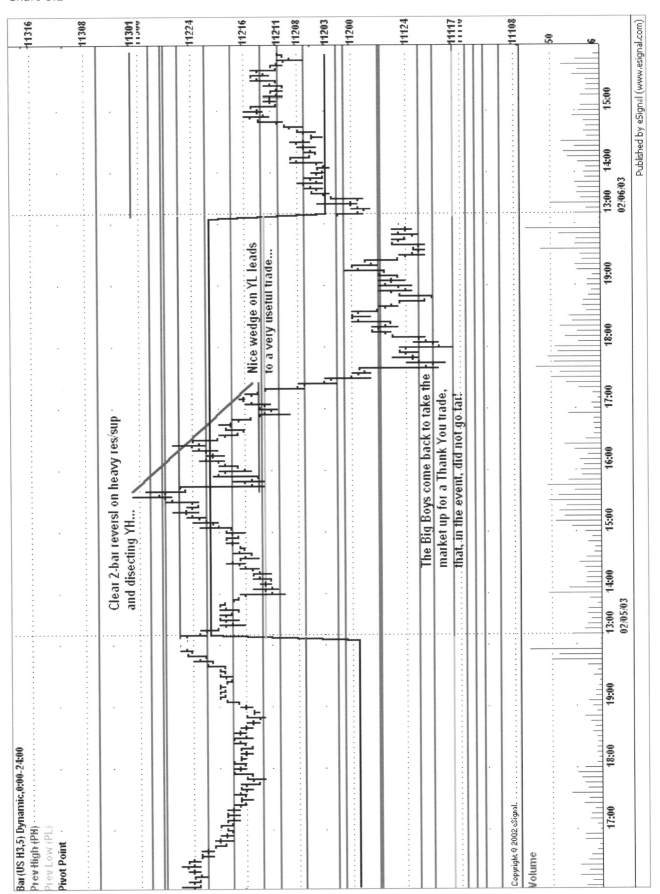

Example – Tell-Tale Gap and J-Hook

With close study you will see that there was a lot of very good information on the chart, before Today started:

1. Yesterday had been a tight range day, for the reasons stated

2. Yesterday had closed on its high

3. There was likely to be a breakout because of the narrow range day and much would depend on where today opened.

4. There was a 7.30 Report

5. If the market went north and could get through the two lots of heavy res/sup after YH, there appeared to be nothing to stop reaching the Contract High

6. If the market went south – in fact, gapped below YL, while it would signal a big down day, it would also have the makings of an Oops trade (to be discussed in the next chapter)

In fact, there looked to be the prospect of good movement… but one cannot second guess or wish, just watch and react. The opening and the report would have led a trader to believe the market was going to head north. The odds certainly looked that way, but the tight range on the three heavy lines of res/sup seemed to be forming a wedge against the odds.

Because of the heavy support underneath, it would be necessary to wait for a break through YH before committing – and then probably for a test of YH afterwards. In fact the market started to rise back and ended with two *Tell-Tale Gaps* and a big bar through the resistance for a super trade up to the CH.

Then, a truly classic *J-Hook* announced the end of the move and a very good Thank You trade down to the close.

Chart 6.3

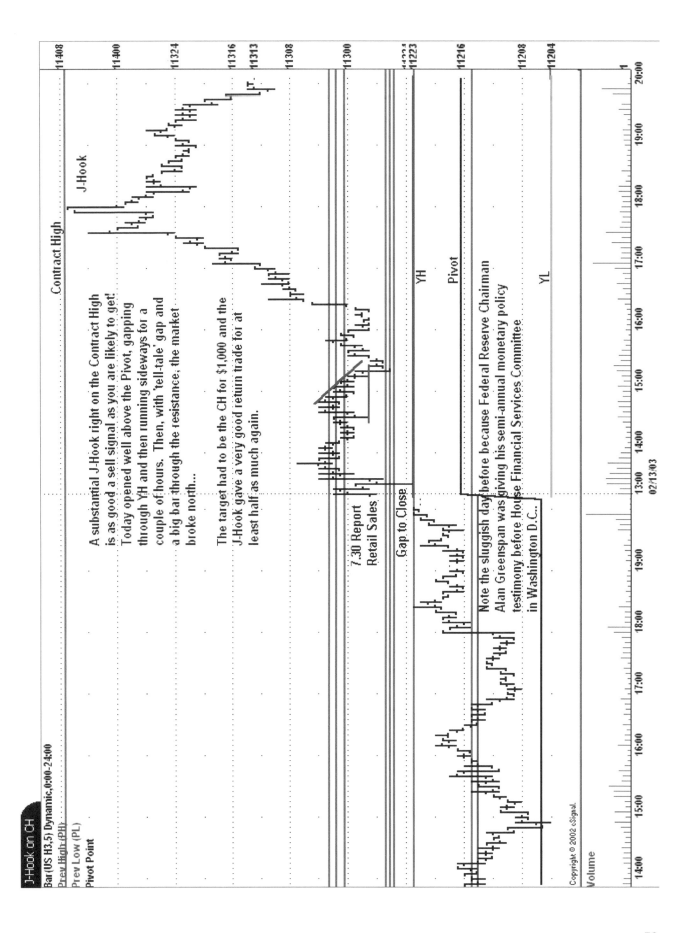

A substantial J-Hook right on the Contract High is as good a sell signal as you are likely to get!

Today opened well above the Pivot, gapping through YH and then running sideways for a couple of hours. Then, with 'tell-tale' gap and a big bar through the resistance, the market broke north...

The target had to be the CH for $1,000 and the J-Hook gave a very good return trade for at least half as much again.

7.30 Report
Retail Sales

Gap to Close

Note the sluggish day before because Federal Reserve Chairman Alan Greenspan was giving his semi-annual monetary policy testimony before House Financial Services Committee in Washington D.C...

Example – Doji Sandwich

The first of these two days involves the announcement of the interest change by the FOMC, following their meeting the previous day. Consequently, you would be warned by the Economic Calendar to keep out of the market from just before 1.15 pm CST.

Today opened with a Gap to Close and after bouncing gently off YH, that was what it proceeded to do – leaving two *Wedges* to get short. The gap then closed with two more *Wedges* against the Pivot. The trouble was that this was the precise time that the Big Boys returned to the pit – and they promptly took it down further. Eventually, the market took out YL, and then retraced back, to close with a *Wedge* in the opposite direction.

Note the time and place of where the *Doji Sandwich* (DS) patterns are and how effective they are in showing you what the market is doing.

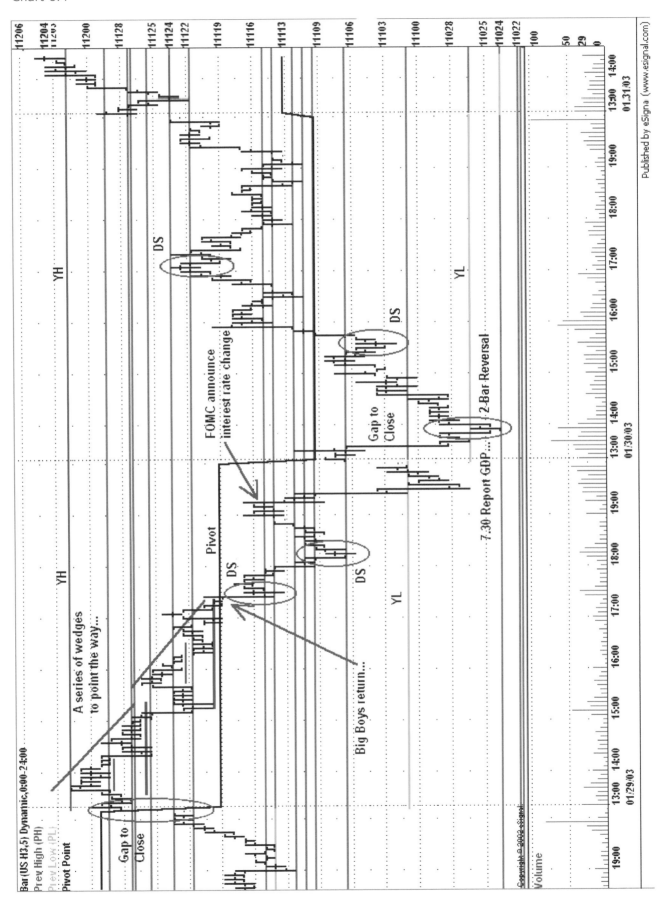

Chart 6.4

Example – Wedges and Failed TTT

Here are two more consecutive days, with the first one starting with a small *Gap to Close* and the 7.30 Report spiking up to YH and then coming off to the Pivot – where it bounced with a *Doji Sandwich*. A good fill would have made a swing trade to YH and the bullish retracement took the market through YH with a big bar – only to go into a small range and back down to YH.

In nine small bars it refused to close below YH and so took the least line of resistance (as the market always does) and start to head north on it original course. The intraday high coincided with the return of the Big Boys, who decided to take the market back down again – indicating their intention with a *Wedge*. The next day opened where it closed and the 7.30 Report took the market back to the Pivot where a *Failed Third Time Through* started another little *Wedge* for a trip down to YL. The retracement was bearish and the start of yet another little *Wedge*, which produced a *TTT* that ended with a spectacular *J-Hook* – to start another good trading possibility which the Big Boys seemed to like the idea of, when they returned at their usual 11.30 CST.

Chart 6.5

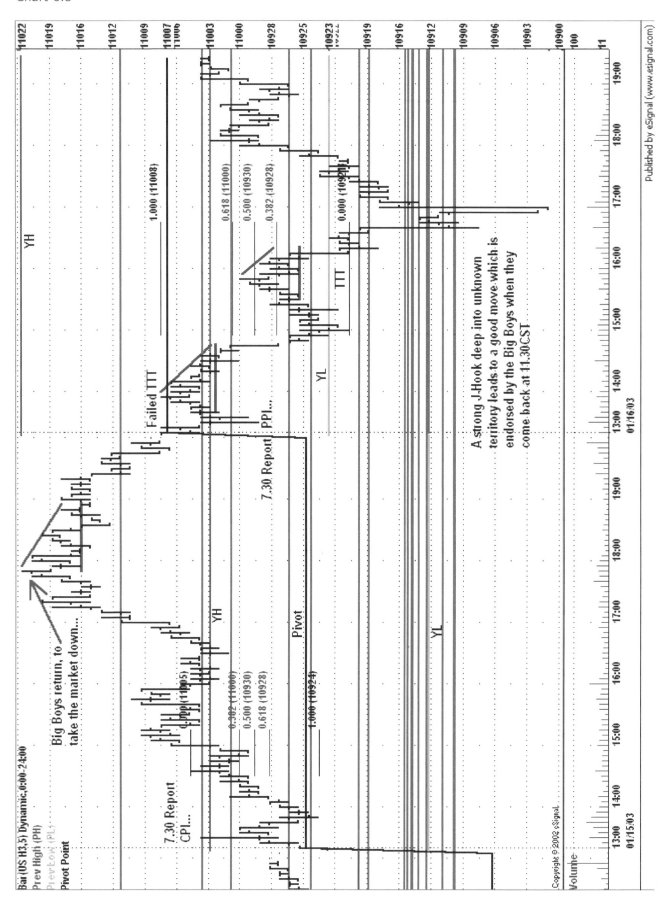

Example – Rounded bottoms and wedges

A big gap up through YH and DBYH would indicate some serious intent to go north, but the first bar started to descend and the next four – with total lack of commitment and failing to take out YH. You would still be looking to buy, but what? Where is the pattern? Slowly, with small bars, it started to build what might be a wedge, but in fact it was a good *Rounded Bottom* ending with a tiny *TTT* followed by a full-bodied *TTT* incorporating a *Tell-Tale Gap.* After that was an excellent move up through the rcs/sup arca to put in a *Doji Sandwich* on the intraday high. Then the Big Boys came back and put in a southerly *Wedge* followed by another one – for a dozen ticks down to the close.

The second day shown, opened with a small *Gap to Close* and started to rise, before forming a small *Wedge* just before the opening bell of the NYSE. If you joined on the first bar down to the Pivot, you picked up a very good windfall down to YL – and took you profit during the very bearish little retracement. The *Downthrust* enveloped in a *Doji Sandwich* would have put anyone long and then when faced with a *J-Hook* on 2DBYH, the reversal down again demanded by the Big Boys would have been a nice ride on their backs!

Chart 6.6

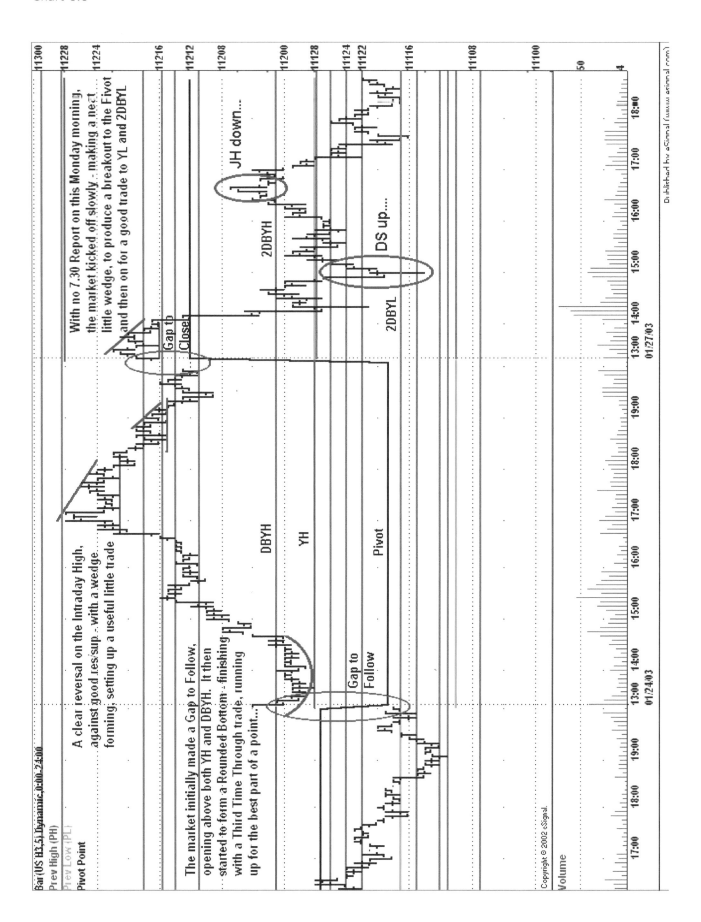

The market initially made a Gap to Follow, opening above both YH and DBYH. It then started to form a Rounded Bottom - finishing with a Third Time Through trade, running up for the best part of a point...

A clear reversal on the Intraday High, against good res/sup - with a wedge forming, setting up a useful little trade

With no 7.30 Report on this Monday morning, the market kicked off slowly - making a neat little wedge, to produce a breakout to the Pivot - and then on for a good trade to YL and 2DBYL

JH down...

DS up....

2DBYH

2DBYL

DBYH

YH

Pivot

Gap to Follow

Gap to Close

Bar (US H3.5) Dynamic, 0:00-24:00
Prev High (PH)
Prev Low (PL)
Pivot Point

Volume

01/24/03   01/27/03

Example – Wedges

Just a cursory look at this chart will show you how much time you would have had to analyse and prepare yourself for this excellent trade south. The build up of the completed *Wedge* was four hours in the making, but you might well have been tempted to get a good fill by joining before the break. In fact, there was plenty of time once it did break and the little retracement would have given you a good fill anyway.

You cannot know how big a move will follow a breakout of a *Wedge*, but as a general rule the larger the formation, the bigger the break. We will discuss the actual trading aspects in a later chapter.

Chart 6.7

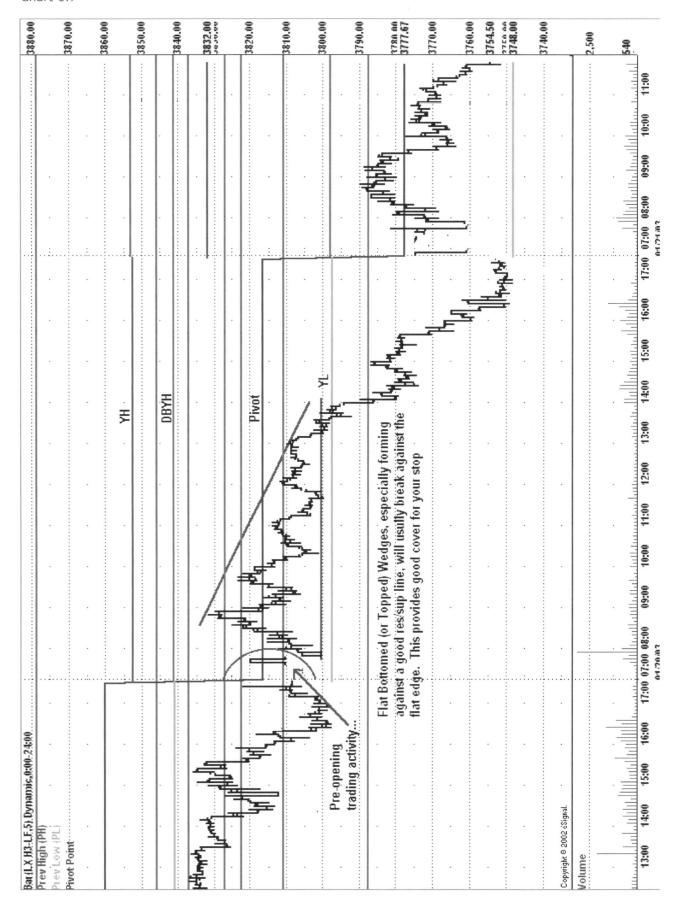

Example – Third Time Through

A *Third Time Through* (TTT) is a good pattern, especially when the market has formed a trading range. Often, the first bar up is at the very beginning and then the second one is towards the end, with the final break obviously at the end. Many such patterns end with a wedge-like formation, in that the bars are forming higher lows as they approach the moment of breaking through. While not in this particular case, the breakthrough bar is often accompanied by a *Tell-Tale Gap* – to give greater impetus to the start of the move.

While this pattern led to a very good trade, ending with an albeit not very tidy looking *Doji Sandwich*, you can also see a *Picking Up Stragglers*, for a secondary entry on the Pivot.

Chart 6.8

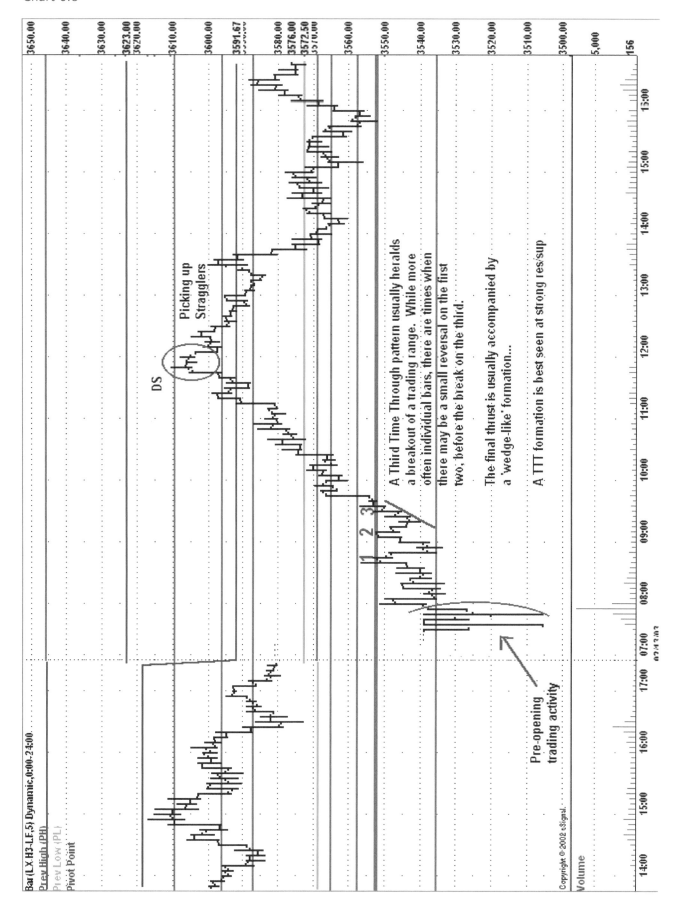

Bar (LX.H3-LF,5) Dynamic,0:00-24:00.
Prev High (PH)
Prev Low (PL)
Pivot Point

Picking up
Stragglers

DS

A Third Time Through pattern usually heralds
a breakout of a trading range. While more
often individual bars, there are times when
there may be a small reversal on the first
two, before the break on the third.

The final thrust is usually accompanied by
a 'wedge-like' formation.

A TTT formation is best seen at strong res/sup

Pre-opening
trading activity

Copyright © 2002 eSignal.

Volume

Example – Rounded tops and bottoms

The *Rounded Top* and *Rounded Bottom* are both very good, but not so frequent, patterns and usually it is best to have one of the confirming charts to the fore, to be able to see them forming. Often, but not always, the middle bar is a doji or an Upthrust and if the end where it breaks is on or close by a decent res/sup line, the better the end result.

In this case, the market opened with a *Gap to Follow* – which, indeed, it did not! – but instead formed a *Rounded Bottom* and started to move towards closing the gap. (You can't win them all!). It then put in a big bar to clear DBYH and, as it subsequently proved, started a *Rounded Top*. If you look on the 13 minute chart, you can see the formation of this pattern quite clearly and on the 5 minute chart there was plenty of time to prepare for the trade – with your stop behind the DBYH line.

To give further encouragement, a nice little *Tell-Tale Gap* appeared just before the Pivot, which was very handy for adding to the position. The Big Boys then came back and took the market further down with a flourish, before feigning a reversal 'on nothing' and then doing so quite loudly a couple of ticks from YL. (Once again the trading aspects will be discussed later on.)

Chart 6.9

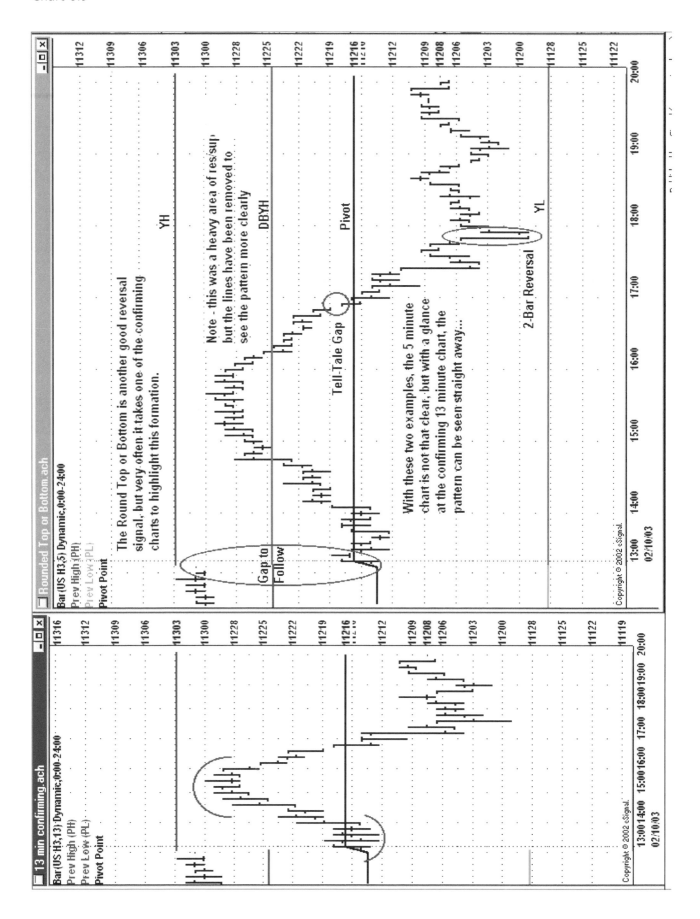

The Round Top or Bottom is another good reversal signal, but very often it takes one of the confirming charts to highlight this formation.

Note - this was a heavy area of res/sup, but the lines have been removed to see the pattern more clearly

With these two examples, the 5 minute chart is not that clear, but with a glance at the confirming 13 minute chart, the pattern can be seen straight away...

65

Example – Rounded top, Tell-Tale Gap and Doji Sandwich

The day after a public holiday in the USA is often a quiet one, but this day did provide a couple of trades, both of which were heralded by accepted price patterns. Having opened with a *Gap to Close*, the market (notwithstanding the minor 7.30 Report) broke through YH but without much enthusiasm, in that it immediately formed a *Rounded Top* and came back through the line. If not aboard the train south immediately, there was a nice *Tell-Tale Gap* to ensure that you got short and tucked your stop behind the res/sup line, conveniently provided!

The target would have to have been YL and 2DBYH, as a powerfully reinforced line – and so it turned out to be. The *Doji Sandwich* reversal provided a good trade north, but the prolonged period of congestion would have had you out with profits before the Big Boys came back.

Chart 6.10

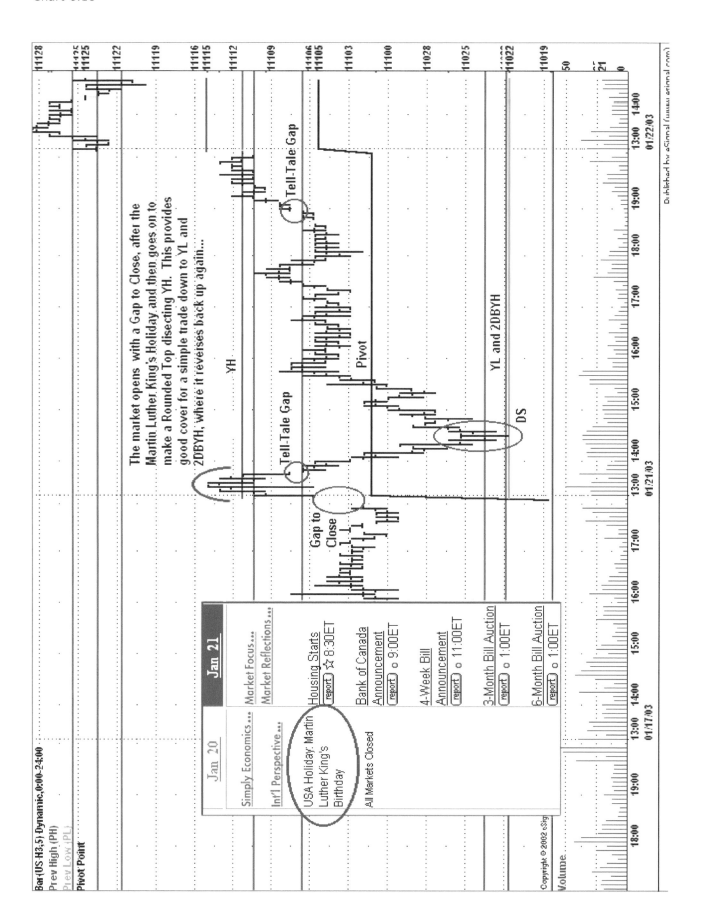

The market opens with a Gap to Close, after the Martin Luther King's Holiday, and then goes on to make a Rounded Top disecting YH. This provides good cover for a simple trade down to YL and 2DBYH, where it reverses back up again...

Conclusion

The price patterns you have been reviewing are by no means a definitive list. In the next chapter you will see others, in and among what I call *formations*, since they are spread over a much broader time scale. But whatever price patterns you see, it is vital to remember that their validity is very much dependent on where they are on the chart and at what time they appear. Furthermore and of considerable importance is the fact that there are a number of other matters that you have to take into account.

Patterns and, as we shall see, other chart formations may well point the way the market is going, but whether or not there is a trade there for you to take, or even prudent if it is possible, is a wholly different matter. Trading is a holistic business and in many ways it is easy to see what has to be done, but very often it is also jolly difficult to do.

Chapter

7

Formations, First Fridays & other phenomena
trends – formations – relationships

While the many price patterns that you have seen in the previous chapter are in current daily use, we now turn to what I call – to make a distinction – *formations*. These are not every day occurrences but are caused by the price action, which in turn then reacts to them. Let's start with the simple trend line.

Trends

The seasoned trader knows all about how to draw a trend line and, once drawn, practically anyone can point to the meaning of it. Whether it shows the market going up, down or sideways, it become abundantly obvious which way it is moving, once the lines are in position. Clearly, with the larger, longer trends there may be counter trends within and perhaps more counter trends within those. The further the market moves, the easier it becomes to see the trends within the trends.

What is not so easy is to do is to predict when and where exactly it is going to breach that trend and start another one. Knowing that, or to be more precise, knowing how to play it when you've spotted it, is nearly always an excellent money making opportunity.

Look at Chart 7.1 opposite and you will see exactly how the bond market has been trending for six months or more. More importantly, you can see exactly where the market breached the line and how the majority were against pivotal res/sup lines.

Trends line have tremendous application, but the power of them is very much allied to the res/sup lines and in the end it is the latter which is the trigger for the day trader. Obviously, it is when the market is approaching the trend lines that they become really interesting, whereas when the market is in the middle it is only if you can determine a counter trend that their usefulness comes back into focus again.

Chart 7.1

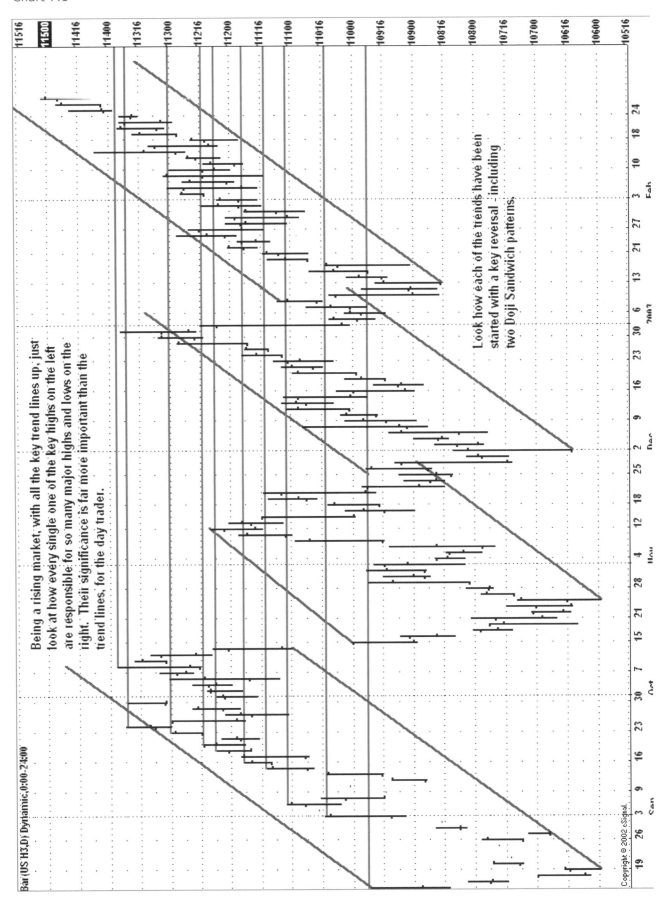

Being a rising market, with all the key trend lines up, just look at how every single one of the key highs on the left are responsible for so many major highs and lows on the right. Their significance is far more important than the trend lines, for the day trader.

Look how each of the trends have been started with a key reversal - including two Doji Sandwich patterns.

Bar (US H3,D) Dynamic,0:00-24:00

Copyright © 2002 eSignal.

71

Now look at the last set of trend lines and see what exactly did happen as the days ahead unfolded and, more importantly, see how you had all the information in front of you to execute a good trade. In Chart 7.2 opposite you will see a larger scale representation of that final section, without all the red res/sup lines – since we are concentrating purely on the effect of the trend lines.

1. The change in trend occurred as the result of a Doji Sandwich although you would not have known the line or angle of the trend at all. The next two bars would have told you that the market looked like being on the up, but the low of the third bar would have got you going with a line – and it would have been parallel to the lower line of the immediate trend to the left. The upper line would have been rising with every high, until such time as you had a retracement (and the position player would have been long all the way!).

2. Until this bar's low was in, you would not really have been able to confirm your lower trend line. It was going up all right, but it might have been starting a broad band of sideways congestion. But once that bar was in, then you had a solid three points to work with – and, using a parallel line tool, could then draw the upper trend line (extended, of course) with some degree of confidence. Then, looking left, you could see very clearly what the market was doing and have been able to play the res/sup lines for your daily trading, within the trend.

3. The market then went on up – pretty much in the middle – reacting well to the res/sup lines, which were gradually getting thinner on the ground because of the new Contract High (CH) which had been put in. Then the market put in some quite large range days, creating even more new CH points, one after the other. You would not have been human, if you didn't think two things, while this mid-trend activity was going on: is the market going to keep on going up and eventually burst through, or is it going to give up mid way through the trend and come down – and out!

4. In the event, as you can see, the market did go on up and almost every day for nearly a fortnight it was creating a stream of CHs. The trend line was holding all the way and then suddenly one morning you wake to a huge Gap to Follow opening (as a huge bounce off the upper trend line) and the writing was on the wall. While you were making a handsome profit on the southerly direction the market had taken, early on you would have had a weather eye open for the market reversing and doing an Oops trade (which we will, indeed, cover next – as we will the Inside Day trade which follows the breather bar the next day).

5. The Gap to Follow after the Inside Day would have put any trader following these patterns long – but not for long! The Rounded Top that then formed would have negated the trade and the exit would have pointed to what turned out to be (not known at the time of course) a truly spectacular trade. Significantly, this large bar cut through the trend line and then closed well below it. The next day, with the test of the trend line, followed by a further Gap to Follow opening tells its own story – especially once you have got the feel for price action trading…

Chart 7.2 – T-Bonds (Feb-Mar 2003)

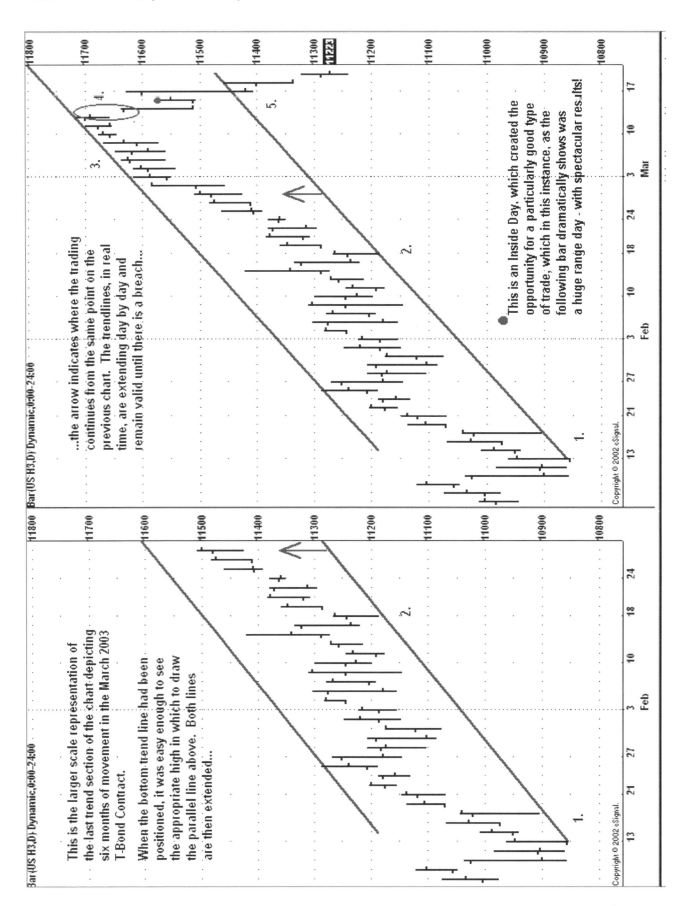

Before moving on, look at the charts again and then note the dates. The whole of the up trend would have been explained by a fundamentalist as the bonds reaction to the plunging stock market, because of the build-up to the Gulf War II. A perfectly reasonable analysis, but I would hate to have had to *trade it* without, as they might say, 'all those wiggles you chaps put on the charts…' When the market was bouncing along underneath the trend line, it would be obvious that something was going to happen. The fundamentalist would have been sure to think that the stocks could not go on down for ever – bear market or no. There simply had to be a rally of some sort. The point was *when*? And what was the *signal to go*? When did you put *money on the line*?

Look at the chart of the FTSE 100 March Contract and you can see how the trend line, combined with the J-Hook was all that was needed to capitalize on the situation. The Tell-Tale Gap the next day was a wonderful indicator that a really strong up move was coming and that a breakout really did look on the cards. Now look at the other aspects on this chart:

1. This high was the bar which allowed you to join the high of the 17 May 2002 at 5367, to make the upper trend line. Then, using the parallel tool bar, you could gently slide the line down to the low of 29th October 2002 to produce the extended lines you are looking at. After that, it was just a question of watching the market come off and meander down the middle of the tram lines.

2. The market slowly rose again until the bounce on the 13 January 2003. Shortly after that was the steady and sustained move down to the lower trend line.

3. The low of 27 January 2003 at 2426 was spot on the trend line, to give even greater credence to the line. So when the next bar was a Doji, then a deep Doji Downthrust, with great confidence you would have been long with the opening the next day – for a fairly volatile ride back again.

4. The market started to come off well before the upper line, only to retrace to within close striking distance of the line on the 3 March 2003, when it put in a stellar bar with a high 3696 – to form the Doji Sandwich for a really solid bounce.

5. Now while the huge down bar stopped well short of the trend line, the big gap opening the next day would have made the astute trader reckon on the bar forming a J-Hook – not by any means the size it turned out to be (but then you are due windfalls every now and then!). The big gap up the following day… and the rest is as already stated!

Chart 7.3 – FTSE100 (Nov 2002 – 2003)

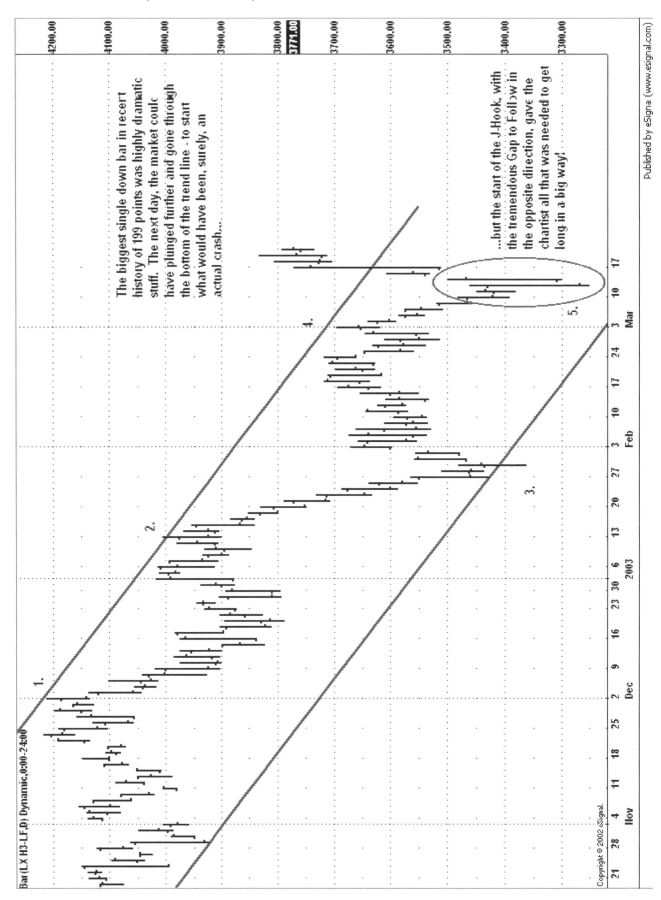

The biggest single down bar in recent history of 199 points was highly dramatic stuff. The next day, the market could have plunged further and gone through the bottom of the trend line - to start what would have been, surely, an actual crash...

...but the start of the J-Hook, with the tremendous Gap to Follow in the opposite direction, gave the chartist all that was needed to get long in a big way!

Bar (LX H3-LF,D) Dynamic,0:00-24:00

Published by eSignal (www.esignal.com)

The Oops trade

In the middle of the last decade, I went to a trading conference in the Bahamas (well, it was February and the thought of lazing about on Paradise Island was a temptation not to be resisted!) and it proved most rewarding because I met the legendary trader Larry Williams. By luck, one of the speakers booked failed to turn up and Larry came along instead. What a character, and I was so pleased to get his book *How I Made $1 Million Last Year Trading Commodities*. Based on his record year in 1973 – when computers were not exactly at their present level of sophistication – there are still some marvelous truisms in it.

Well, this *Oops Trade* which we are going to look at, is all as a result of his personal observation that if Today's market opened below YL and traded back to YL, then you should buy YL. A really simple formula. A really simple opportunity. And a really good track record. (And for those of you whose minds race ahead when they hear a good thing, no it doesn't seem to work ' if the market opens above YH and trades back to YH…') Anyway, take a look at these examples.

As soon as the market closes very near the lows you know there is a chance of starting the next day with an Oops Trade possibility. How far it gaps will, of course, be a factor as will the strength and whereabouts of the support and resistance.

1. With the FTSE (at least on E-Signal) there is this phenomenon of the pre-opening trading activity, which gives a clue as to where the open will be and what might happen directly afterwards. On this day, the market did, indeed, gap down to very near some strong res/sup lines, which it soon gave up trying to go through, providing the opportunity to go long with excellent cover for one's stop.

2. After a couple of hours of a broad band of congestion, the market started to put in a series of higher lows in a wedge-like pattern, producing a clear entry point for the more aggressive trader.

3. The market then ran up in close order to YL and went through in a single bar – with no follow-up retracement or test. The market then went on up to the Pivot and 1DBYH, where it put in a 2-bar reversal pattern, which would have been the place to take profits and watch the retracement.

4. If you were still long, this Doji Sandwich against res/sup would have had you out and the Picking Up Stragglers would have been just the ticket for the southerly trip – allowing for a weather-eye on the time for the opening of the bonds, if the logical target of YL was not achieved.

5. The exit for the bonds opening would have meant also standing aside for the 7.30 Retail Sales Report and seeing exactly what effect it had. The two large bars down would have dictated any further trade to be around YL for entry and stop placement.

Chart 7.4 – Oops trade

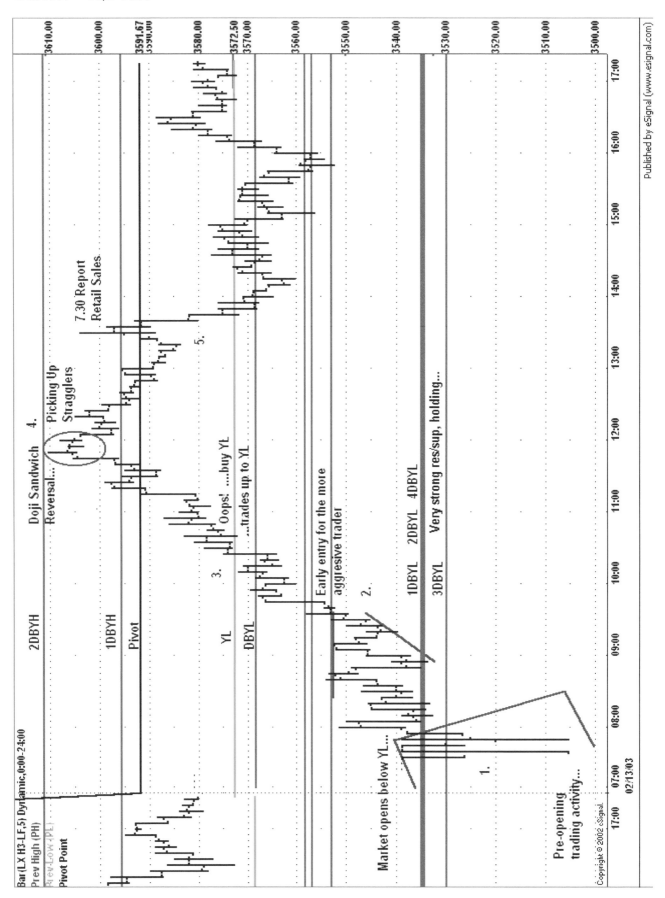

The chart opposite is an interesting example of an Oops Trade, not least because it took a long time to trade back to YL. Most of these trades take off pretty quickly and then the market either goes through YL or backs off pretty quickly. As has been repeatedly said before, with all patterns, every aspect of time and place has to be taken into account – and you have to trade what you see, not what you think the market ought to be doing.

1. The gap opening has immediately given rise to the possibility of an Oops trade, but the market is just above solid support and is looking to make a wedge to go 'the wrong way' according to expectation. In fact, the 9.00 am Consumer Confidence Report has provided the opportunity to break through with a mini-TTT.

2. Without any clear pattern, the market decided to return and then put in yet another wedge to break south. The determination to break through the res/sup lines again may well have got you into a trade – particularly on the test with the small 2-bar reversal – although the proximity of the return of the Big Boys may well have stayed your hand. The day certainly seemed to be becoming choppy and the report did not seem to put direction into the market.

3. When the Big Boys returned they put the market on a northerly course and you would have had a losing trade if you had waited to have your stop taken out. But, if you then joined in the fray in the res/sup area of where the wedges to your left had been formed, a mini TTT presented itself on the line to aim for YL.

4. If you had got into a trade north to YL, you would have simply waited to see if it was going to break through or offer a clear reversal off the line. The sort of bull flag would have held your attention, but the chances are you would have lost patience with the upthrust and come out. But in the next three bars the market was knocking on the door again and this time there was the possibility of an (imperfect?) TTT to buy. At that hour, you might well be out of it, sipping a drink – if not, it was a nice little trade to MOC.

The Oops Trade was certainly a well spotted concept by Larry Williams and he would be the first to tell you – as indeed he did me! – that they don't work all the time. But the potential of the trade, as you start the day always brings a certain sense of excitement – even if it has to be tempered by the actual price action working against you and appearing to dash your hopes.

Chart 7.5 – Oops trade

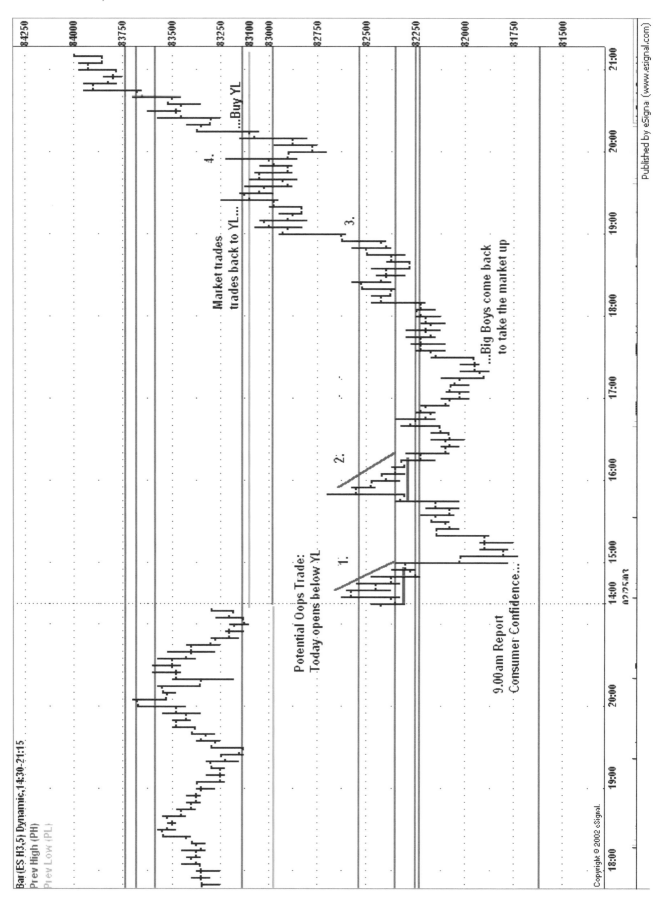

Head and Shoulders

This is one of the very well known formations, but it does not set up that often in the daily run of the T-Bonds. However, Chart 7.6 opposite of the March 2003 contract for the E-Minis is a near perfect example of this very reliable formation.

A cautionary tale of beans

Actually, I have to say that whenever I see a H&S chart it reminds me of a time when, in my early days of trading on the American markets. I was long (with an option or three) September Soybeans and expecting, as my then broker thought, "Beans in the Teens!"

It was August and the harvest had not taken place yet, but my broker in Chicago who dealt with a lot of farmers, was keeping a keen eye on the soil condition. Despite the fact that various crop surveys suggested it was going to be a bumper harvest, he, my broker, had visited many acres personally and knew that the plants were withering where they stood. The crop reports, he suggested, were way too optimistic. "You wait and see," he pleaded, "the price of beans will be in the teens this year." A young friend of mine, who shared the same broker, loaded himself to the gunwhales with calls and we both waited – watching the price descend down the right Shoulder. The Plunger, as my young friend (who went on to trade the S&P 500) became known as, bought even more calls as the price went lower. We both strongly believed that our broker held, as you might say, the inner line of communication on the Beannies!

We were so blinded by the fundamental knowledge of the broker that we totally failed to see the Head & Shoulders formation forming. By the time the price had reached the neckline our calls were showing a major loss. Puts were becoming expensive, but I did manage to off-set my position, slightly. The Plunger bit his lip for too long and by the time he covered he was five figures worth out of pocket. My puts just saved my bacon and I finally got out of the debacle with a few hundred dollars to the good – but that was a wonderful lesson on fundamentals versus technical analysis. It was also a lesson which proved the old adage 'a broker makes you broker' and that, at the end of the day, you must only, but only, make your own decisions, based on your own knowledge. You cannot be reliant on anyone else's opinion.

Chart 7.6 – E-Mini, Head & Shoulders

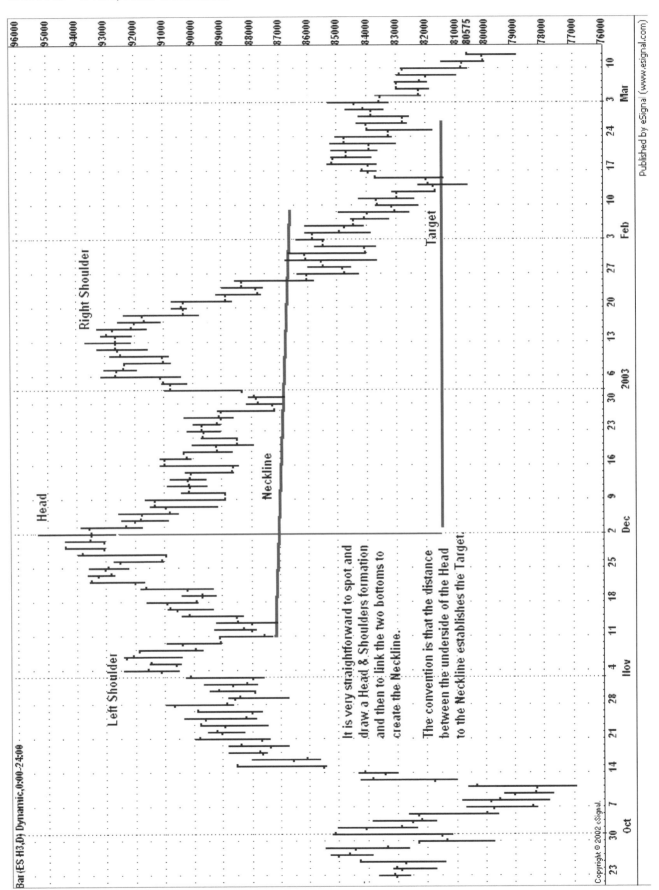

It is very straightforward to spot and draw a Head & Shoulders formation and then to link the two bottoms to create the Neckline.

The convention is that the distance between the underside of the Head to the Neckline establishes the Target.

Inside Day

The Inside Day trade is one of the more reliable formations on the T-bonds. However, like all the others, not perfect by any means, but played carefully it can often turn up some marvellous trades. Sometimes easy to trade, sometimes not . . .

Inside Day

Chart 7.7 – Inside Day

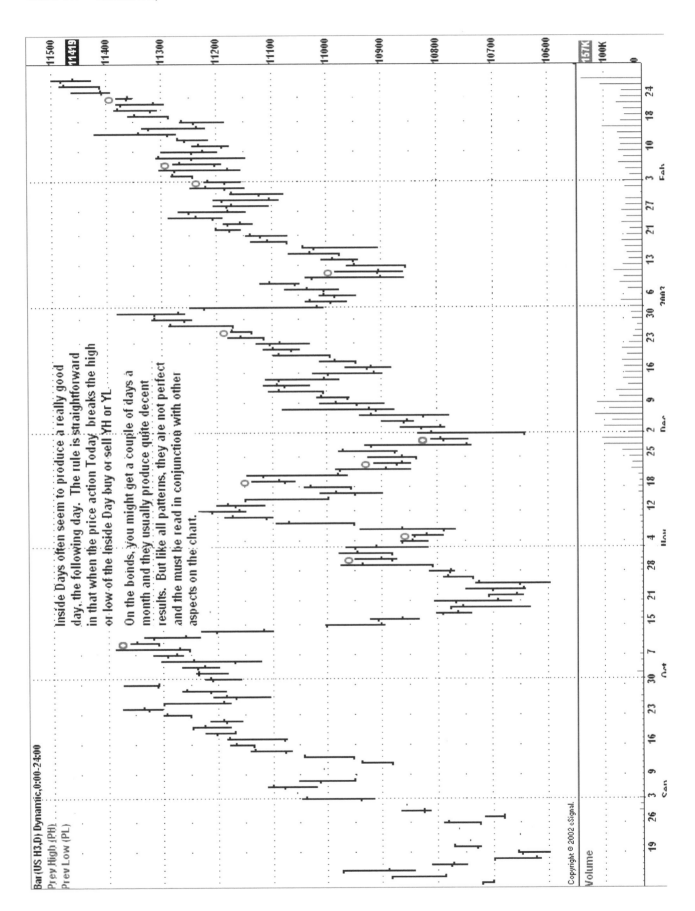

Inside Days often seem to produce a really good day, the following day. The rule is straightforward in that when the price action Today, breaks the high or low of the Inside Day buy or sell YH or YL.

On the bonds, you might get a couple of days a month and they usually produce quite decent results. But like all patterns, they are not perfect and the must be read in conjunction with other aspects on the chart.

In the first example of the Inside Day opposite, the market opened with a Gap to Follow, which went right through YH, so the expectation would be for an up day. But the market went immediately sideways for four bars and then formed a Rounded Top as a complete reversal. Perverse maybe, but the market is always right!

What was fortunate in this case was that heading south instead of north would be more likely to produce a better trade, if it took out YL, which in the end it did – and how. The big bar down proved the point and the small doji after it provided the entry. The move then took off with another good down bar, which, incidentally, I call a Continuation Doji Sandwich. These can be see anywhere in the middle of a move and usually, but not reliably, indicate that there is still some way to go before exhaustion.

As soon as the market crossed back over YH, the target immediately became YL and the bearish retracement from the Pivot confirmed that we were on our way. There was, of course, no way of knowing how far the market would go, but it turned into a very nice windfall.

Chart 7.8 – Inside Day - example 1

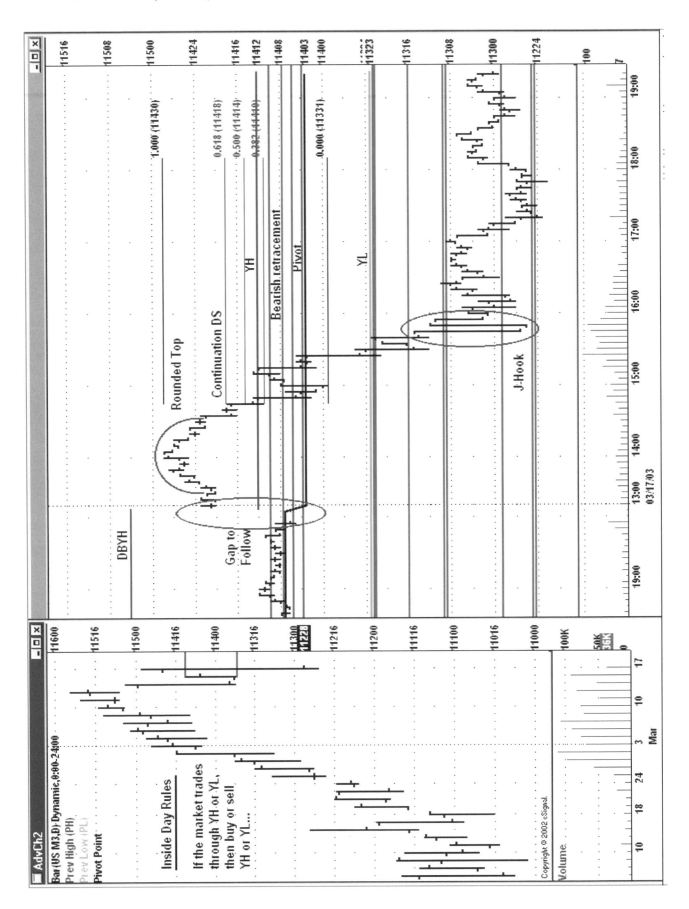

Turning now to another example shown in Chart 7.9 opposite, which also opened with a Gap to Follow and did, indeed, stay above YH all day; nevertheless, it was a difficult one to trade, as you will see – not least because the T-Bond March 2003 contract was going through a period of producing a whole series of new Contract Highs and this Inside Day trade was also to the north!

1. Having opened with a large Gap to Follow, the market then proceeded to hit the Contract High and much as one would have liked to join it in the break to make yet another CH, it would have been prudent to withdraw for the 7.55 Redbook Report. Not noted for bringing in extreme volatility into the market, the Big Boys could equally have used the occasion to have gone directly south – for the same swing against you. The retracement was barely bullish, again, you would have had to withdraw for the up coming report.

2. The 9.00am Consumer Confidence Report can be a good volatility maker and you would have had to see that it really had turned on the 'next' CH. Just how many ticks you would have made and where your stop would have been against exactly what target, with what risk/reward computation, you can come back to after you have absorbed the next chapter. Suffice it to say there was very solid resistance ahead in the form of the original CH, which in the end it broke through with gusto.

3. The 2-bar reversal/retracement on the intraday low poses a similar question, particularly in relation to the cover for your stop. As always, during this move up – if you had been aboard – you would have been conscious about the return of the Big Boys, who, in the event, decided to bring the market down again. The best target, bearing in mind the solid res/sup lines around 113^26, would have allowed you to squeeze a 3:1 trade, with a good fill from and your stop behind the original CH (before Today started). Not an easy day to trade.

Summary of Inside Day trades

Inside Day trades can be very good, but you have to be aware of the trading circumstances surrounding it. Big gaps, rather than trading through the line, unfortunately, eat into the potential profit and the lack of res/sup lines makes it more difficult to secure your cover. These days happen and the rule must be not to gamble through frustration.

Chart 7.9 – Inside Day - example 2

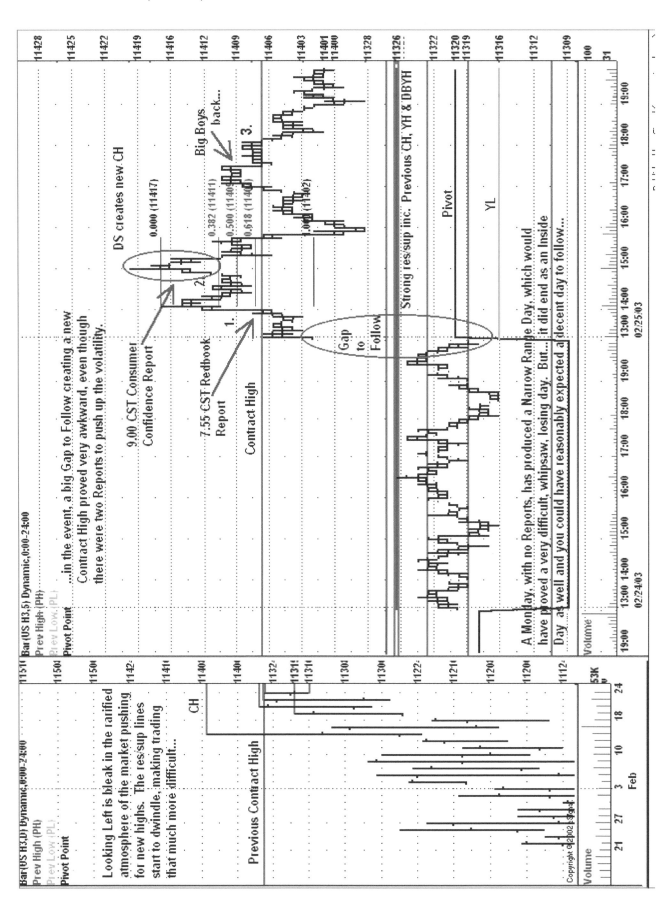

First Fridays

With rare exceptions, the first Friday of every month is the set day for what is called *The Employment Situation*. It always used to be called the *Unemployment Numbers* or the *Nonfarm Payroll Employment* figures. The talking heads on CNBC have themselves a field day with such lovely phrases as "the employment data continues to disappoint . . . data is weaker than expected . . . markets continue to be mesmerised by . . ." etc. Whatever is said, the moment the Report is actually announced, at precisely 7.30 am CST, the market goes mad. The madness can last for several minutes, with huge swings in all directions and the volatility getting really pumped up. Then, after it has settled down, the market usually takes stock of itself and starts trending solidly in one direction. Played carefully, the day can often produce spectacular results.

Opposite, and on page 88 are a couple of good examples of First Friday trading.

Chart 7.10 – Trading a First Friday - example 1

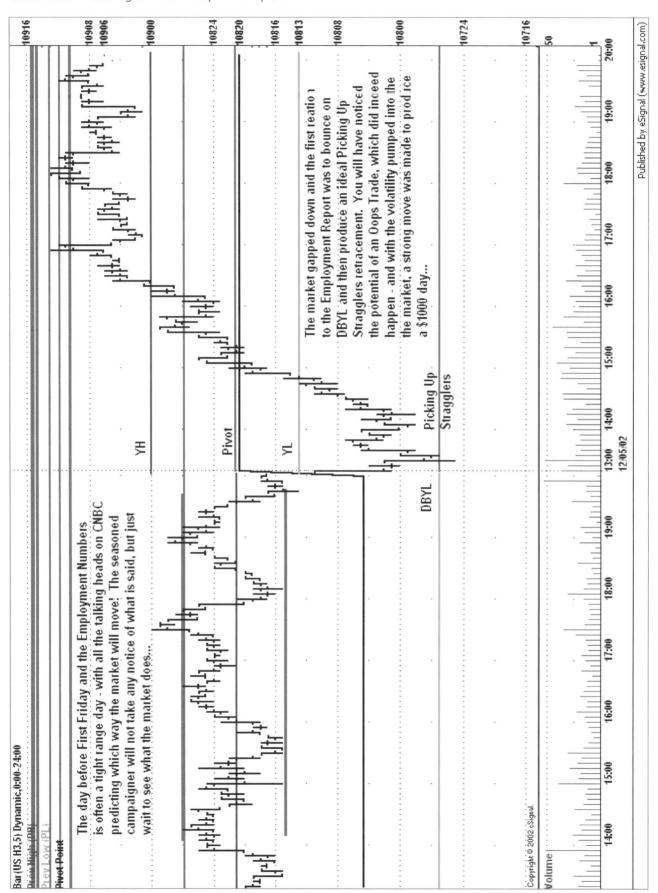

The day before First Friday and the Employment Numbers is often a tight range day - with all the talking heads on CNBC predicting which way the market will move! The seasoned campaigner will not take any notice of what is said, but just wait to see what the market does...

The market gapped down and the first reaction to the Employment Report was to bounce on DBYL and then produce an ideal Picking Up Stragglers retracement. You will have noticed the potential of an Oops Trade, which did indeed happen - and with the volatility pumped into the market, a strong move was made to produce a $1000 day...

Published by eSignal (www.esignal.com)

Chart 7.11 – Trading a First Friday - example 2

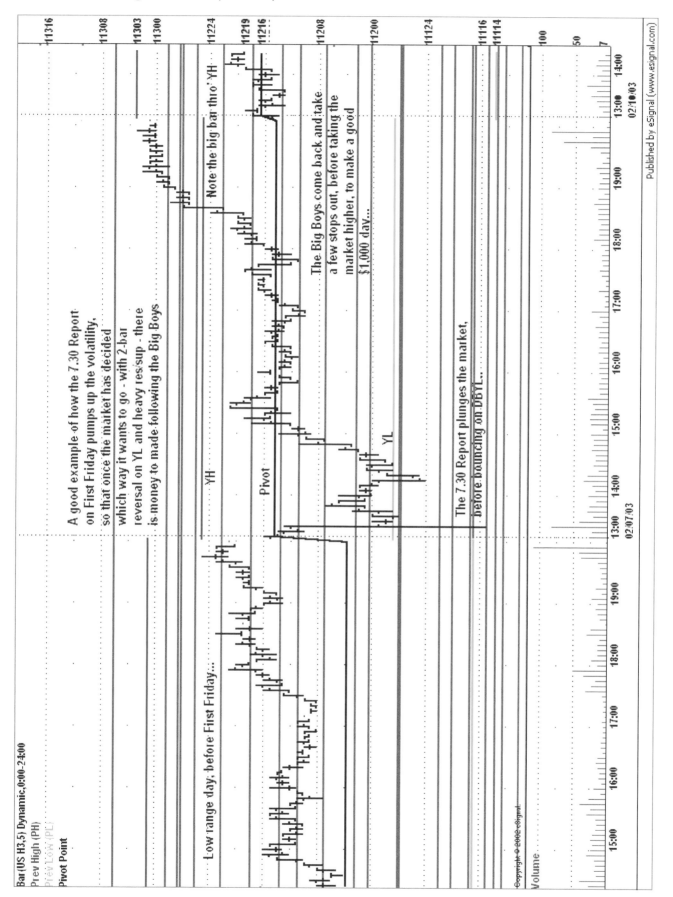

A good example of how the 7.30 Report on First Friday pumps up the volatility, so that once the market has decided which way it wants to go - with 2-bar reversal on YL and heavy res/sup - there is money to made following the Big Boys

Note the big bar thro' YH

YH

Pivot

The Big Boys come back and take a few stops out, before taking the market higher, to make a good $1,000 day...

YL

The 7.30 Report plunges the market, before bouncing on DBTL...

Low range day, before First Friday...

Bar (US H3,5) Dynamic, 0:00-24:00
Prev High (PH)
Prev Low (PL)
Pivot Point

Volume

Published by eSignal (www.esignal.com)

Contract relationship

Almost whatever you trade you will find one or more contracts which either run in step or else are totally the opposite. For example, whatever the New York Stock Exchange does, so too does the London Stock Exchange. If the Dow goes up, the FTSE goes up, the Dow goes down, the FTSE goes down. All the time. In fact the only time they get out of kilter is when America is sleeping and England has woken up five hours ahead and is vainly trying to trade without holding onto Uncle Sam's coattails!

For those who appreciate the facts, it is always laughable to hear the so-called experts and pundits reflecting on the television on what made the FTSE go up or down – as if on its own – rather than because the Dow led the way. Furthermore, it is not just that the market goes the same way, it does so from bar to bar. The only difference usually is in the magnitude or otherwise of the bar.

So far as the bonds are concerned, there was a time when they too were in step and actually led the stocks. However, for the last several years they have become totally the opposite. Now when stocks go up, bonds go down and vice versa. The result of all of this is an extremely interesting 'indicator' for the observant trader. Take a look at the chart I have prepared (Chart 7.12) based on the price action for a good volatile day, like First Friday, March 2003.

As you can see, the FTSE and S&P are virtually hand in hand, even though the size of the bar may differ, while the bonds are diametrically opposed to both of them. You really need to watch a live chart to see how each tick relates to each other. Certainly there are times when the S&P will make a move up and the bonds appear to have been caught napping – not for long, but sometimes long enough to get a trade on *knowing* that events are going to catch up. Naturally, you have to be careful and make sure that the trade you take is still consistent with all the other facets of the market that have to come together as part of your decision making process.

This is why it is important when you trade the bonds to keep a close eye on what the Spoo is doing. Actually, since the E-Mini moves in *exactly* the same way as the S&P, tick by tick, if you are not actually going to trade that instrument, you can subscribe just a nominal exchange fee for the E-Mini, rather than its elder sister. If there were any discrepancies and it compromised your knowledge vis-à-vis boos and spoos, I would not suggest it!

Chart 7.12

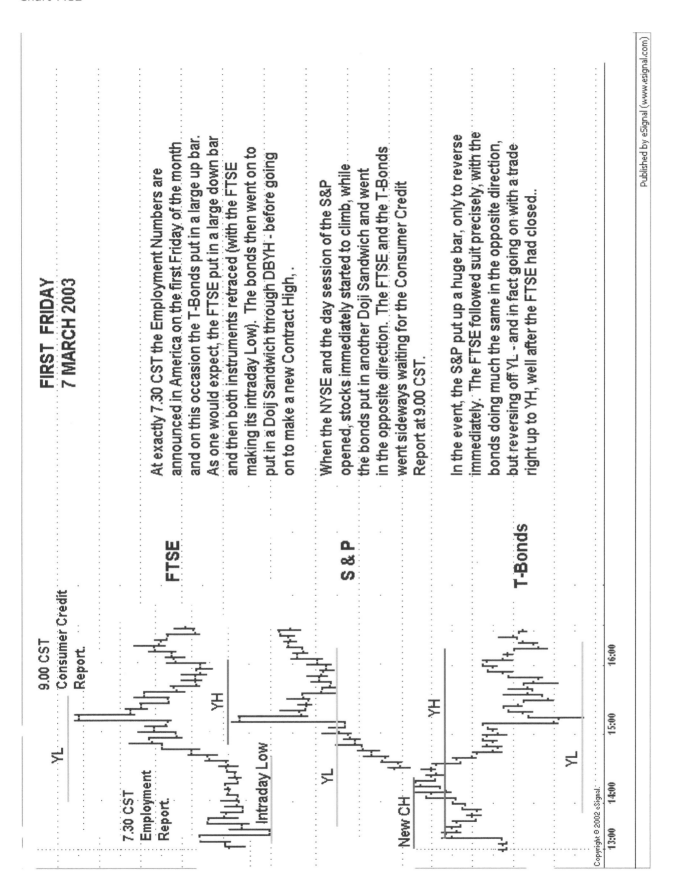

**FIRST FRIDAY
7 MARCH 2003**

At exactly 7.30 CST the Employment Numbers are announced in America on the first Friday of the month and on this occasion the T-Bonds put in a large up bar. As one would expect, the FTSE put in a large down bar and then both instruments retraced (with the FTSE making its intraday Low). The bonds then went on to put in a Doji Sandwich through DBYH - before going on to make a new Contract High, .

When the NYSE and the day session of the S&P opened, stocks immediately started to climb, while the bonds put in another Doji Sandwich and went in the opposite direction. The FTSE and the T-Bonds went sideways waiting for the Consumer Credit Report at 9.00 CST.

In the event, the S&P put up a huge bar, only to reverse immediately. The FTSE followed suit precisely, with the bonds doing much the same in the opposite direction, but reversing off YL - and in fact going on with a trade right up to YH, well after the FTSE had closed..

93

Pre-Opening Trading Activity

This is a strange but useful phenomenon and goes to prove that all sorts of little things can help give yourself an edge, if you happen to recognise the value when you stumble across them. For reasons best known to LIFFE and E-Signal the pre-opening trading activity on the FTSE Futures are sent out by the exchange and the data feed company, even though they are not trades. They are, as I understand it, just bids and offers which are being placed prior to the opening and most will be cancelled on opening. However, they do give an indication of what the thinking is and as you can see from Chart 7.13 opposite, as well as from Chart 7.4 on page 75, the pre-opening activity is very useful.

Obviously, it is not going to be as reliable as the official overnight trading on the S&P and the T-Bonds, but it is a daily occurrence and long may it last. It is important to note that you must, when measuring any retracements, measure from the 'true' high or low and not including the pre-opening activity. Fortunately, the automatic 'previous day's high and low' lines provide by E-Signal do take the 'true' price for the calculation and drawing the next day.

It is not a big deal, but I think you will find a useful little indicator to have on hand as you do your own pre-opening non-trading activity.

Chart 7.13

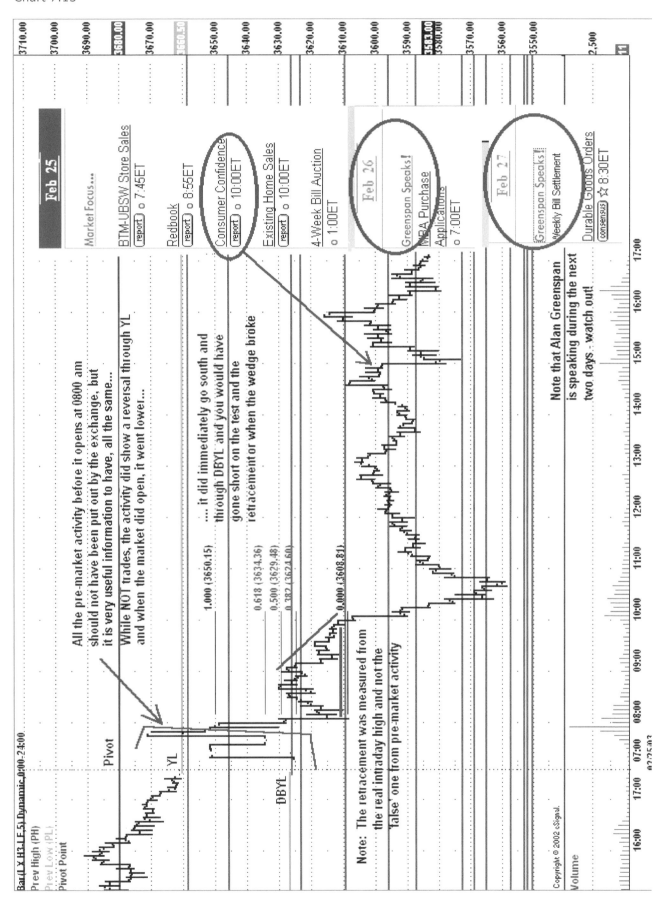

Gap Openings

Whilst you have seen the mention of Gap Openings in the previous chapter and have seen examples of this phenomenon, you should be aware of the 'rule' as it applies to the bonds. By the very nature of things, it is the size of the gap that counts and very often where the market has actually gapped to, is another part of the equation.

Like all the other patterns, they do not work out as expected all the time, but having said that, you will find that the price patterns that follow a gap will very often determine what happens next. So far as a closing gap is concerned, it does provide a target for the market (and the trader!). Chart 7.14 gives illustrations of the three types of gaps and the approximate tick values which should be assigned to the individual type. While the *Gap to Close* is based more or less on an average swing in the bonds, the *Gap to Follow* is usually a considerable gap – and one that demonstrates which way the market is wanting to go. Obviously, the Either Way gap is the most difficult to forecast accurately, and in all cases you have to judge according to the immediate price action following and the market environment in which it is happening.

Chart 7.14

OPENING GAPS

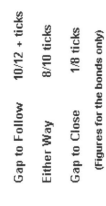

Gap to Follow	10/12 + ticks
Either Way	8/10 ticks
Gap to Close	1/8 ticks

(Figures for the bonds only)

1. The market opened with a good gap to follow, including a little Picking Up Stragglers retracement, for late entry.

2. An either way gap that opened on nearby resistance then made a solid downthrust which might have closed the gap straight away. The reversal in the single bar foretold the move and the Picking Up Stragglers confirmed it.

3. A small gap opening soon turned into a nice little wedge in the opposite direction - to give notice of the move to come.

Chapter 8

Risk/Reward ratio

calculation – entry – stops – targets – exits

Now we come to the vital subject of money management – which at the end of the day is what makes or breaks the whole trading effort. You can look left, set out the res/sup lines, see the patterns, use your Fibonacci tool, take account of the formations and generally do everything you should do, to be able to read the market, but - and it is an important but - you will get nowhere without a really good money management system.

It is impossible to be able to read the market and get it right all the time. There is no Holy Grail system. The very best you can do is to make more money on your winning trades than you lose on your losing trades – after all commissions, expenses, etc have been deducted. Unless you are a genius, you are going to have more trades where you either lose or come out quits than you have winning trades and so you must have some means of putting the odds in your favour. You need what the professionals call an edge. Difficult? Of course! Can do? *Poss-eee-blé*, as might be said in the land of vines and olive groves that I like to frequent in Andalucia.

There are many books and papers on money management containing all sorts of higher maths. Assuredly there are programs that can be written, spreadsheets that can be used and a host of other computer technicalities incorporated into a trading plan. Fine. But I am a great believer in keeping things simple and maths in particular – no doubt because all my life I have been a great deal more literate than I ever have been numerate. In fact, I understand completely why my mathematics master at school wrote in despair at my failing to have even the least understanding of calculus, "…he has reached the *pons asinorum* – the bridge at which the ass will not cross."

As you must have appreciated by now, price action trading has nothing to do with maths (except for Fibonacci), but everything to do with observation and interpretation. It is a very human occupation and, as such, it is essential to allow for getting it wrong rather more often than getting it right. It is all a question of reading the market and trying to let the profits run from point to point, while cutting one's losses at a more precise point.

So . . . having done you homework on the market, as it is moving along and you spot what you think is a trade, based on all the factors we have been discussing, you have to assess:

1.	the **point of entry**
2.	the **stop**
3.	the **target**

and most important of all

4.	the **risk/reward ratio** (which, to give you the sort of edge you need, you will find should not be less than 3:1.

Look at the charts on the following pages and on each one you will see the points above marked.

Example 1 – Risk/reward

Observations on Chart 8.1

1. Having seen a huge J-Hook reaching to within a tick of YH and creating the intraday high, you decide that the market must be going south. During the latter stages of the formation of the bar, you would have had two or three minutes to assess what fill you might get, where your stop ought to be and where your target must be for a minimum 3:1 trade.

2. There are two res/sup lines close together and if you could get a fill at 111^19, then a stop at 111^22 would be quite satisfactory.

3. Your first target would have logically been the intraday low at 111^08 and the next, more solid res/sup line to aim for would be YL a 111^00 even. That is probably far enough to look at that time.

4. The risk/reward of the first target would be11 ticks from entry to target, so with your stop say 3 ticks away, the target would be easily over 3:1 and the second target 19 ticks, yielding a risk/reward/ratio (r/r/r) of 6:1.

Twenty minutes later a big bar takes you through the Pivot and it looks as if you are going to make the first target quite easily. The market then goes on down and looks as if it is going to hit YL, but it misses by a tick. You now have to decide whether you take the profits on the table, hold for what would certainly be a retracement or that the next bar will keep up the momentum and go through. It is easy to say with hindsight, but the reality is that you immediately put up your Fib tool, saw the .500 line was the Pivot and came out a couple of bars later with a dozen ticks under your belt. (Depending on how you trade, you might well have taken profits to put you in the clear at the intraday low and may well have brought your stop up to it.)

Whether you held the retracement, re-joined at the Pivot or the intraday low, you would have had a wary eye open for the return of the Big Boys at 11.30 CST. Whatever you did you would have been out as the bar crossed the YL and waited to see what the market was going to do.

For the purpose of this exercise, forget the potential of the counter trend trade, but appreciate that the J-Hook reaching to the original intraday low target is precisely on the very bearish .382 (not shown, so as not to overload the chart) In those circumstances you might well have said to yourself, if the market goes through YL *again* then if you tuck your stop directly behind the line and can get a fill of only one or two ticks away, the trade would only have to go to one or the other of the two other arrows – pointing to a r/r/r of 3:1 and 6:1 from YL

What I hope you will appreciate is that there is very good time to come to the decision you want to take and that, within the concept of my price action trading, the information you need is available before the event. Had the trades not gone according to plan you should not have lost more than the r/r/r you were using.

Turn the page to see another one.

Chart 8.1 – Risk/reward - example 1

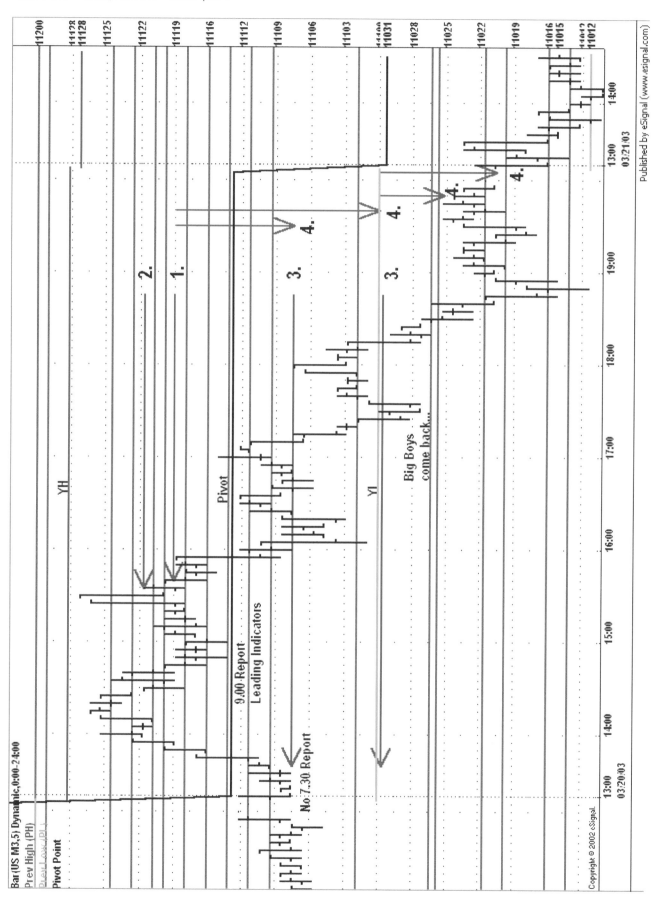

Example 2 – Risk/reward

This chart contains two days: on the left hand one the market had some volatility pumped into it by the 9.00 Wholesale Trade Report, which made it bounce within a tick of its DBYL and then move up through YH to create a new CH. The market then made a bullish retracement to bounce off this CH, just before the Big Boys came back. Using the same numbered sequence as the second day, see how you would have traded the move up and the one down. Meanwhile, this day had its effect being 'on the left' of the next day and here are the points numerated:

Observations on Chart 8.2

1. The day started with an Either Way Gap and bounced straight off the previous day's new Contract High – to produce a trade that you may work out to be a great deal less than it looks at first sight. However the bounce off YL would have allowed and entry at 115^10 – or the same price as Picking Up Stragglers, which in the circumstances of having no reports, might have been the best option..

2. The stop would have had to be behind YL at115^05, as the nearest res/sup for cover.

3. The target would be YH or the intraday high and the new CH. Any thing less would not have had a 3:1 r/r/r/. Bearing in mind that the market had already been there that day, it was not unreasonable to think it might return. – but the Fib tool would have been out all the way, to make sure it was not a retracement off YL.

4. The r/r/r would have been just over 3:1, but it was a half big point trade (16 ticks) in fairly rarified atmosphere. If the entry was as Picking Up Stragglers, you would have seen 1DBYH breached already and once past DBYH, the bullish retracement would have allowed you to bring your stop up to the Pivot or 1DBYH.

It really is important to do this exercise every time before you put on a trade. The target has to be realistic, within the scope of the day. If the trade is not there and the r/r/r is wrong, it is only going to lead to trouble. The first trade of the day (as you will no doubt have worked out by now) could have been excellent if you were very fast and had got filled early in the third bar – with your stop tucked up under the new CH. Otherwise you would have had to wait for the wedge to form just under DBYH and have then had some difficulty getting out with many ticks in your pocket, notwithstanding having only just squeezed a 3:1 r/r/r in the first place.

Consider this one now . . .

Chart 8.2 – Risk/reward - example 2

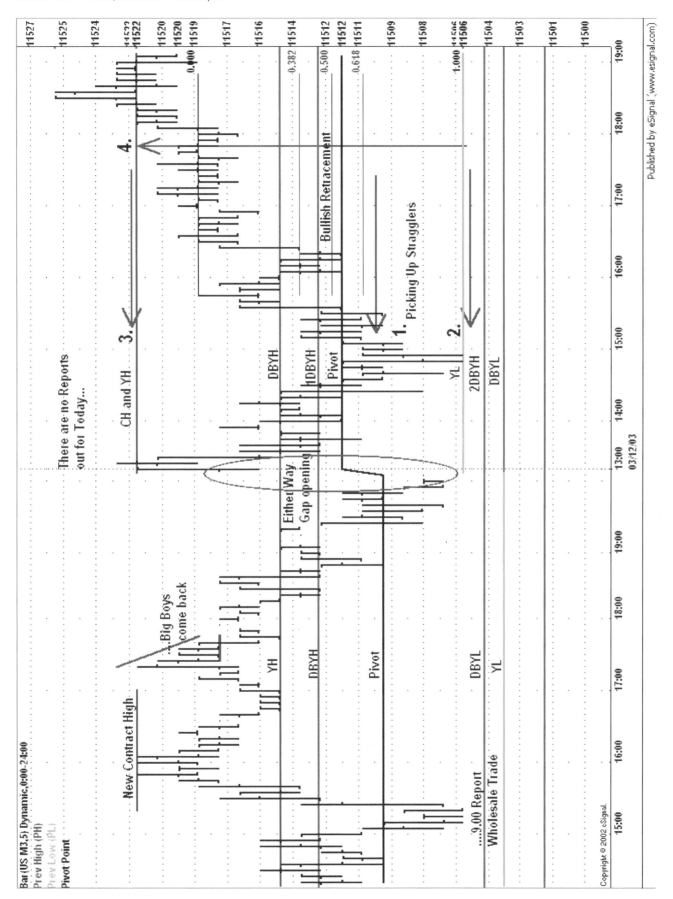

Example 3 – Risk/reward

Another chart with two consecutive days, so that you can have a go at the first one and see what you make of it. The main clues are there, in between the only res/sup lines current in the rarified atmosphere of the market making new highs. So far as the second day is concerned, the 9.00 Report pushed the market down and you might have caught a trade as it went through 2DBYH – tucking your stop behind it for a 3 or 4:1 r/r/r. In the event, you would have had to cover with the downthrust/DS for not as much profit as you hoped.

But...

1. The combination pattern of a downthrust/DS within a Rounded Bottom would have had you working   out how you could best get into a long trade. You should at least have got a fill at 114^12 – but if you waited for Stragglers you would have been disappointed and had to accept 2DBYH for entry, with your stop behind it.

2. To have got in at 114^12 your stop would have had to be behind YL at114^07, so you would be looking for a multiplication of 5 to find the appropriate target.

3. The mathematics would demand a target of 15 ticks, which would take you to DBYH. Since that is where the market descended from, it would not be an unreasonable thought. With the mood the market had been in (which you would know from looking left!) the CH and YH could easily be taken out for a secondary target.

4. So the entry, stop and target looks good and the final stage would be to confirm the r/r/r before pressing the button. A five tick stop for 15 ticks to target – good. Once passed 2DBYH stop could be brought up (or if forced to delay entry until then, the r/r/r to target would be even better – for less profit!

In the event, the target was exceeded and while you would have taken profits (depending on how many contracts you trade) you would have let the trade run to the CH and YH – being careful to be out for the return of the Big Boys, who brought the market down with a tempting wedge for a nice Thank You trade, which is so much their hallmark.

Chart 8.3 – Risk/reward - example 3

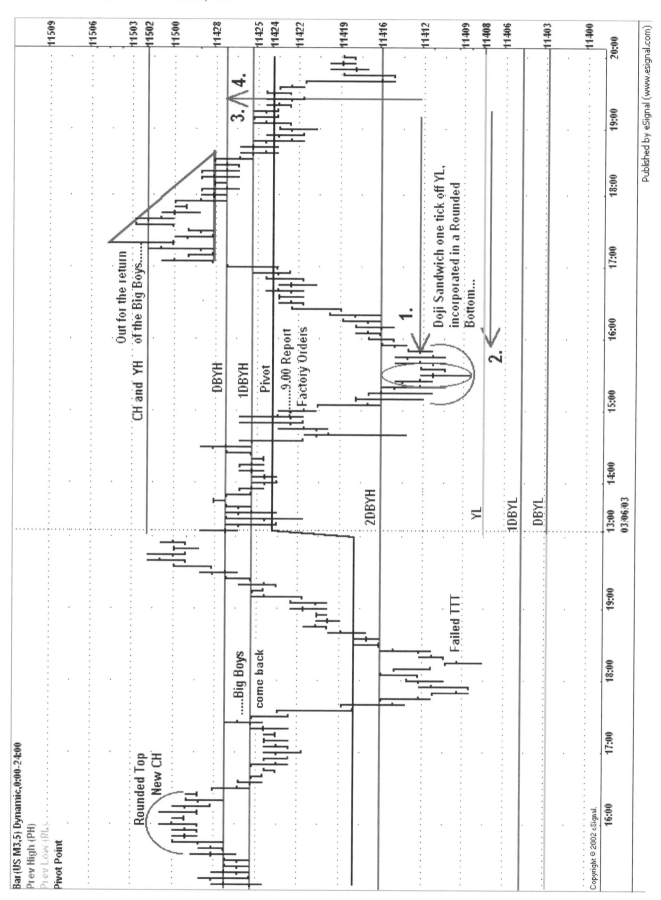

Example – First Friday trade

The next example is a First Friday trade and while with hindsight it must seem perfectly obvious how to have traded it, life is never so kind when you are on the leading edge, actually watching the price action and having to pull the trigger.

The first bar after the report was huge. Straight up, with not even a hint of taking the stops out, as it can so often do. The small doji before the report halted on DBYH and the first movement from the report might well have been down, to take out the stops before going north. Clearly the Big Boys just wanted to get on with it in rapid fashion. The bar completed a Doji Sandwich on DBYH and an aggressive trader might have joined the fun on the opening of the next bar (expecting a TTT, perhaps?). Anyway, the next was almost a small doji, followed by the continuation, then a couple of smaller bars – closing off their highs.

Then we get the first down bar and the market showing some signs of stalling. So, for half an hour or more you have simply watched with amazement from the sidelines. Then you will start to detect the formation of a small wedge. The first signs of a top? Will it be retracement? Is it the beginnings of a reversal? These are the questions which will be going through your mind. So, what do you do?

The first thing to do, of course, is to put up the Fibonacci tool and see how the move stacks up. You would notice that the first line, the .382 is coinciding with the doji bar on the way up and bang on a res/sup line. If it is going to be a bullish retracement, then this may be as far as it is going to go down. That is about 12 ticks away from the res/sup line on the bottom of the wedge. Get a good fill and run a 3 or 4 tick stop for an acceptable trade.

The next, .500 line, is on the start of some pretty solid looking res/sup lines, which the market will have to get through, if it is going to go on down. Perhaps that will be as far as the market will retrace? That would be quite a good run and may offer an even better trade back up to the intraday high. Finally, you look at the .618 retracement in between res/sup and if it goes through there, well you can reasonably think of YL as the target. That's a $1,000 trade… and the market will have produced what I call a *Fountain Hills* – named after the world's tallest man-made fountain, which I saw, while visiting my elder daughter who lived not far from the fashionable resort of Scotsdale in Arizona. It is quite magnificent the way the water is driven powerfully into the blue, blue sky and then free-falls back like the white plumes of a general's cocked hat on Horse Guards.

While there would be no way you could have known that the market was going to do such a major reversal, you would have covered your steps all along the way. You would do this by bringing up your stop to lock in and/or take profits, depending on the number of contracts that you trade. So, to summarize against the numbers on the chart:

Observations on Chart 8.4

1. The first big bar through the wedge ended on the highs and you would probably have waited for the start of the second. If you had waited until the end you would have had to use the next res/sup line, as it gapped through. If you waited for Stragglers, you would never have made the trade – at least until the .382 line.

2. There was good cover for your stop, for both the early entry or the secondary one – and you would be moving your stop down, as the market progressed.

3. You would not have realistically have made this your target from the top. As discussed you would be looking at the Fibonacci retracements and using the clusters of res/sup lines.

3. Your initial maths would have related to the .382 line, with re-calcs along the way down, as you secured your stop.

Chart 8.4 – Risk/reward - example 4

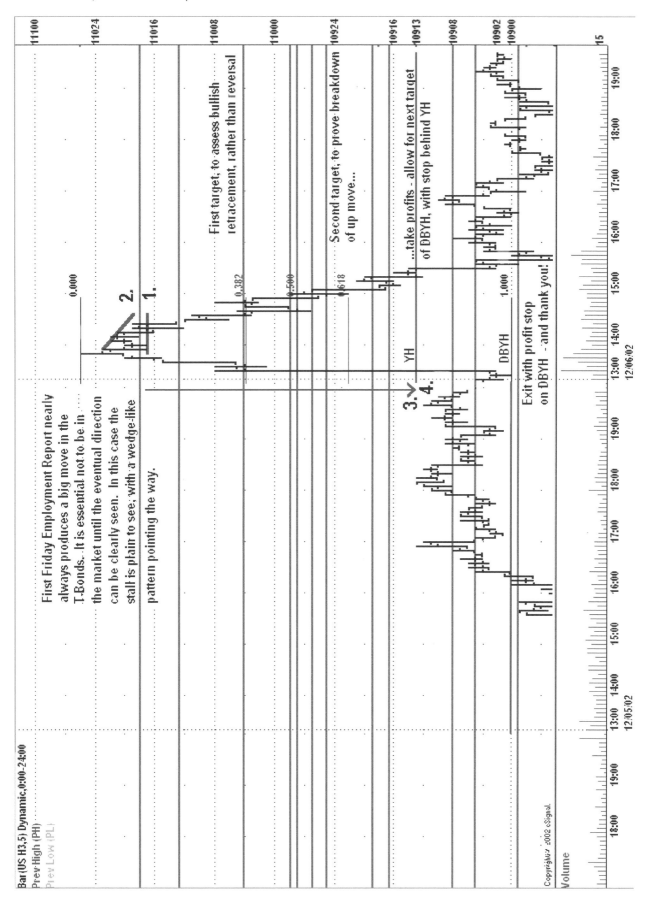

First Friday Employment Report nearly always produces a big move in the T-Bonds. It is essential not to be in the market until the eventual direction can be clearly seen. In this case the stall is plain to see, with a wedge-like pattern pointing the way.

First target, to assess bullish retracement, rather than reversal

Second target, to prove breakdown of up move...

...take profits - allow for next target of DBYH, with stop behind YH

Exit with profit stop on DBYH - and thank you!

Bar (US H3,5) Dynamic, 0:00-24:00
Prev High (PH)
Prev Low (PL)

0.000

0.382

0.500

.618

1.000

YH

DBYH

Volume

In trading a day like this, when the volatility has been pumped up really high, the one thing that you would feel – quite rightly – was that the market would make a decent move. Obviously, the whole move might well have been in the rapid rise from the report and the market might then have simply 'waved a flag from the masthead' as I call it, when it does. But it didn't! The main thing is that you would have had the time to assess the situation and get it right and if you had bought and not sold the wedge, you would have had to cover with a loss of about 8 ticks – and then pick up the trail again.

At no time did the market put in a reversal pattern to have had you covering your position. So you would have just stayed short until the obvious stall, after having seen it reverse, cutting DBYH. But, most traders would have said a very big thank you and exited, counting their blessings and their cash when it first hit DBYH. $1,000 days need to be banked!

Low-risk learning

Using spread betting to learn price action trading

There is no doubt that those learning to trade or learning to trade a new instrument or learning to trade in a new manner or with a new system, can pay a heavy price for their mistakes. In the conventional way, through a recognized stock or futures broker, buying shares or futures' contracts requires an account being backed by a substantial amount of money, as well as trading in multiple units of shares or heavily geared futures contracts. It is the professional way that business on the stock exchanges and futures markets is carried out.

Any seasoned trader will understand that the markets are run by and for the members of those markets. The participants are the professionals and, while they certainly trade their own account, they are primarily there to trade on behalf of their clients. At the end of the day, you are but one of many clients and the only room for negotiation you have is over the commissions you pay. Whether you trade through the broker or directly to the pits via the internet or satellite, you are an outsider, using the services provided by the exchange and its members. It is very much a "you and they" situation.

There are no concessions for beginners. You can paper trade and we all know the limited value in that, for those who are really new to trading. Most people appreciate that you have to put your money on the line, you have to feel the pain, let alone get the gain! As legendary trader Jesse Livermore said, "You can't tell till you bet!" The sad thing is that there is no university degree in trading, there is no school to learn the skills (except perhaps for some courses or seminars put together by traders). For most people, there seems to be no other way than stumping up the capital and having a go. Consequently, many would-be excellent traders get wiped out before they ever really have a chance to prove themselves.

But now, at least in the UK, there is a way of learning the business without having to risk all. There is a sensible – if not perfect way, as you will see – of stepping into the arena and seeing whether or not trading is for you. Or, in this case, whether the concept of price action trading the bonds is for you – or not. By the way, I believe that Americans and others can use the internet based companies in the UK, but where they stand in so far as the taxation situation in their own countries is concerned, is another matter. The reasons for showing how spread betting can be used as a tool for learning to trade, is purely not to be killed by the trading cost in the conventional manner.

So, what is spread betting? How does it work? And, more importantly, how does it work for the newbie wanting to get to grips with the price action trading method.

Spread Betting

> *'Spread betting is a flexible and tax-efficient alternative to conventional dealing in futures markets, stock markets and currencies.'*

This is the opening line of the brochure of IG Index, who go on to describe themselves as, "Britain's leading financial bookmaker." The key word there is *bookmaker*.

With spread betting your business is not with a broker, but rather a bookmaker and while both, in essence, do the same job for you, as their client, in respect of dealing, the big difference is the way they each earn their corn out of you.

- **The Broker** agrees a rate of commission with you dependent on the number of deals or the contracts you trade. It is entirely up to him, in relation to what you are prepared to accept.

- **The Bookmaker** makes no commission out of you, because all his costs and profits are made out of the bid/ask spread, which he sets for each of the instruments you are trading.

The result is that, with the broker you pay tax according to your earnings, but with the bookmaker you actually pay no tax at all (because the business is treated as gambling, which is exempt CGT). Now, paying no tax may sound very good, but you have to remember that you only pay tax on the profits – and you have to make a profit first. This, you might find rather more difficult with the spread being set by the firm, according to their needs, rather than the market itself, according to the way it is moving (which has nothing to do with the broker!) You must appreciate that –

- The **broker** is only allowed to accept orders for contracts, as per and in accordance with the rules of the exchange concerned. In the bonds, each contract trades for $32.25 per tick. Whatever the bid/ask spread was, for each tick that the underlying instrument moves, you are responsible for $32.25 for each tick it moves – up or down, irrespective of which side of the market you are on. In order to be able to trade a single contract, let alone several, you have to put up substantial margin. This can amount to a large sum of money – certainly for only one or two contracts, the broker is going to ask for £25/£50,000 in your account.

- The **bookmaker**, on the other hand, only trades contracts for the firm's account, as a hedge against the money the client is actually betting. The individual client doesn't trade in contracts, just money. They can bet as little as £2 on telephone orders and perhaps as little as a quarter of that for trades over the internet. There is a lot of difference between $32 or $64 or $96 per tick to trade three contracts and say £2 or £4 or £6 to trade as if you were trading one, two or three contracts.

All this needs careful consideration and study because the service and the spreads can vary from firm to firm. For example, in its printed literature IG Index says that its spread on the bonds is 6 ticks, whereas another firm, Financial Spreads, says that its spread is 4 ticks, so you should shop around. It is important to know what sort of initial training you can get in this new art of spread betting – Finspreads.com, as they are called on their internet site, run a free eight week Training Academy for their clients, where you can trade for as little as a penny a point.

Anyway, there are half a dozen firms out there, for you to choose from, but obviously none of them is going to be offering you the normal *actual* spread in the market, which in the case of the bonds is usually just one tick. But that is beside the point, because your focus must be on learning and practicing price action trading, not on making money, per se.

Example 1 – Spread betting

Look at the chart opposite and let us suppose that you saw a wedge-like formation building on YL . . .

Observations on Chart 9.1

1. You would be looking for a break of the intraday low on YL and when you see a TTT set up you would be doing your home-work on entry, stop, target and r/r/r. With a normal broker, the fill you might expect would be what you are looking at on your screen. If you were doing it with a bookmaker, you could be expecting a 6 tick spread.

2. The trade takes off as you expected and you hold for the retracement.

3. Being anxious that the retracement turns into a bearish one, you lose sight of time and suddenly the market tells you loudly and clearly that you have completely forgotten (you must have know from your initial research before Today started) the 9.00 Report.

4. Having learnt to get out quickly, you react accordingly and manage, during the course of the second bar up, to cover at 111^22. The spread the broker would have given you was just one more tick at ^23 and the bookmaker would have given you three ticks at ^25.

Either way, you would have had a good wake up call concerning reports and resolve to have some alarm system on your computer for 7.30 and 9.00 and vow to be more careful. Clearly, you lost a lesser number of ticks with the broker, but such is the huge difference in trading in units of £2 as opposed to $32, you would have saved a great deal of money with the spread betting firm(a loss of £22 against a loss of over $224 with a broker). Here is a day of mixed fortunes, but one which you should have come out on top and see for yourself the difference in the two methods of trading . . . and learning.

Chart 9.1 – Spread betting - example 1

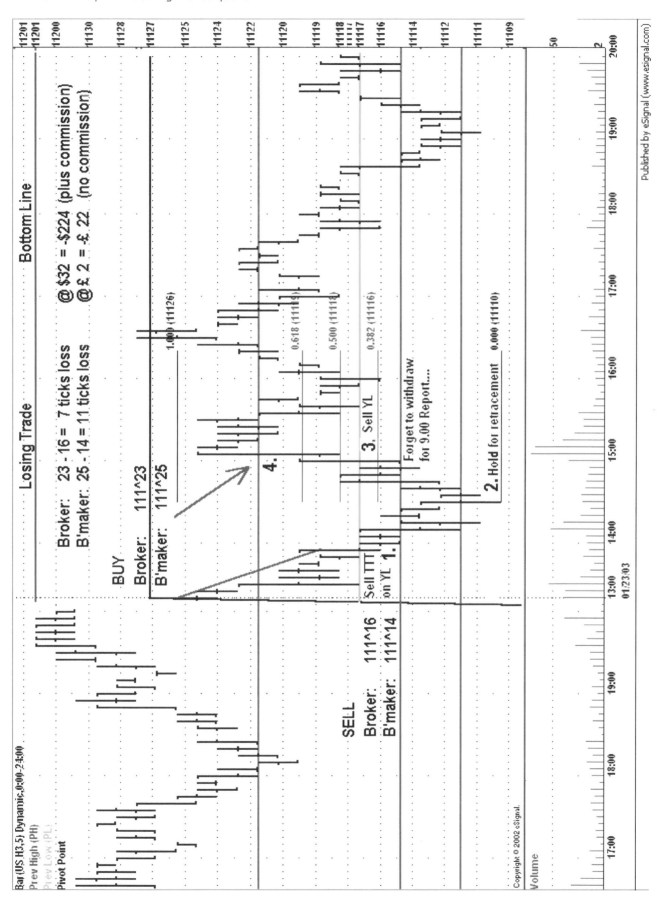

Example 2 – Spread betting

Observations on Chart 9.2

1. Looking at the nearby resistance before the market opened, you might well have thought that the 7.30 Report would bounce on the solid wealds of red, but you would have to wait and see if the volatility would get through the two solid res/sup lines below – as well as YL.

2. The opening of the NYSE and the big 2 bar reversal back through YL would have had you following suit and at that stage you might have thought you had seen the low of the day.

3. The big down bar would have had your Fibonacci tool out and would have soon shown you a .618 on YL (not enough room to show on the chart) and you would have been lucky not to have been in a losing trade, as you covered. Can't win 'em all!

4. However, you would have seen the potential of a TTT through the intraday low and, as the big bar opened below YL, you might well have tucked you stop behind it and pressed the button to descend into the four close lines of res/sup.

5. Once again, you would be getting out the Fibonacci tool and have been relieved to see a bearish retracement and an equally big bar following through. Then, up pops a Doji Downthrust and you would have certainly taken profits or exited – and the Fibonacci tool would be out again!

6. Now a wedge starts to form and if you held for the retracement you would be very pleased. You might reasonably conclude that it was going to be a down day after all! If out and watching, you would be preparing for a likely flat bottom on the Doji resistance line – and you were off again!

7. The market now seems to be stalling and the bars are getting smaller and tighter – and another little wedge is about to form! You would not have caught the move, and in any case the Big Boys on the brink of coming back would have been a major inhibitor …

Most people on this side of the water would be sipping their first of the evening when the Failed TTT showed itself. Excellent cover for your stop and you would have been out at the merest hint of a reversal – like that little Doji on the hill, which turned out to be the middle of the sandwich you were meant to have, as you said *Thank You* to the Big Boys!

As a seasoned trader you can soon work out the sort of day you would have had and the amount of money you would have made on margin with the broker. Also, you can see how much less you would have made trading very conservatively with the bookmaker – but how very little you risked, while you were finding out, learning, practicing, whatever, and perhaps not having the smooth running day that has been portrayed.

From a trading point of view, the only difference with a Spread Betting firm, is that you get 'bad fills' as it were, but save an awful lot of money – against the inevitable mistakes – while you are learning. Furthermore, instead of having to put up a large amount of money for the account, you could get away with as little as 64 times the amount of money you are going to trade (£2 per point perhaps). Rather a different picture for your learning curve, m'thinks, than most seasoned traders had in their early days!

Clearly, those with very limited capital, which they are unwilling or plain unable to commit to a broker's account, will find the concept of trading with a bookmaker a very real option.

Chart 9.2 – Spread betting - example 2

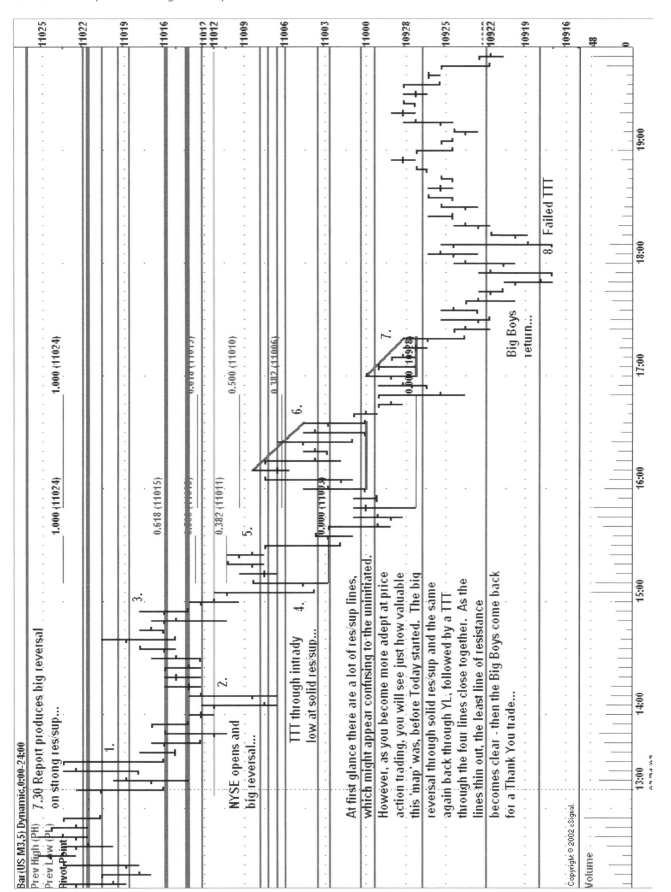

10

Doing it all off PAT!

price action trading – the compleat trader

Having got to this last chapter, you will hopefully be able to see that it is entirely possible to learn to read the tape. Learn *Price Action Trading*. You will appreciate the need to do a lot of homework before the market opens; be able to lay out your map for Today. Recognize the patterns and different formations and what they mean, when spotted against resistance and support. Be able to follow the price against the Fibonacci tool, in order to assess the viability or otherwise of the move you are in or contemplating taking. Then, when you really think that everything is in place, be able to assess the entry point, where the stop ought to be, what the target is and, most important of all, see that the risk/reward ratio makes it all worth the candle. In fact, to be able to understand and do what has to be done in the markets every day, as a price action trader.

As you know, when it comes to trading, anything can happen. Let's face it, you could just be the unlucky one who crosses the street, as it were, just as a mad bull charges round the corner. But it is not very likely, as your experience of crossing streets will tell you. But hundreds of people *are* killed every day on streets all over the world. Life and living is a risk. At least with trading you can try and quantify the risk, you can assess the risk/reward before you start. You can protect your back. You can put yourself in the situation of winning more than when you lose.

The fact is that you can extract money out of the 30-year Treasury Bonds, in the manner in which you have seen, as you have absorbed this book. The potential is there, the possibilities are there, the probabilities are there – all because of the vast liquidity and sheer size of the T-Bond market. The fact that it is so large, so fluid and made up of such a vast and divergent crowd, you can get lost in it, to make a profit. But it is not easy, that is for sure. There is nothing definite about it. It does require a certain *je ne sais quoi* which can only be developed over time. As a result, it is essential to be able to try out all the techniques – at an affordable cost. Thus, the wonderful innovation of spread betting can be a real boon for the beginner and, if need be, a real boon to be able to do it all, if the capital is not there.

Throughout the previous chapters of the book, you have seen particular examples of specific aspects of trading; selective days have been used to make the point. In actual fact, what I have done as I have progressed, is to update the charts as I have gone along, in order to make them wherever possible, as current as they can be – given the parameters of the trading platform provided by E-Signal. Clearly certain types of price patterns remain the same in whatever time frame, day, month or whenever, so all I have tried to show you are really good examples, mainly in the five minute frame, as that is the one you will most use. But, when all is said and done, once you have seen a particular price pattern, it will always be the same. A J-Hook is a J-Hook is a J-Hook. You just have to recognize the pattern and assess its significance, at that time, according to its position within the price action as a whole.

So, as you would expect in a final chapter of a book of this sort, let us review just what price action trading is all about. Just what are the main ingredients involved in putting the whole thing together. Can you really *learn it off PAT*? I hope so.

Before Today starts

It is absolutely impossible to rush in late, sit down, switch on the computer and expect to be able to trade. You have to do preliminary work. It is vital. Quite a bit of it can certainly be done at the ending of Today, if you are not too exhausted and have the time. However, certain things have to wait for the overnight trading to have taken place, for the reaction to any events in Asia and other markets to make themselves felt, before the open of the day session of the bonds (although naturally such things affect the overnight of this instrument, in any case).

The bonds start trading in the UK at 1.20pm and you need to have had lunch and got yourself sorted out, with all your charts up-to-date and everything ready for the opening bell. Just think of those poor souls west of Chicago who have to get up at God knows what hour and be as equally bright eyed and bushy tailed as you are! Still, they get down to the beach early in California!

Opposite is a table of the things you must do and, as a seasoned trader, will no doubt already do – just even more thoroughly:

As they say in instruction manuals when some caveat is required to let them off the hook, "this list in not exhaustive" and it is up to you to check that your work station is in all respects ready for you to start trading.

Things to do before starting

1.	**Re-boot your computer** and make sure the screen(s) are clean.
2.	Check your **internet connection** is working, the computer program is up and running and that the data feed is on-line and streaming.
3.	Make sure the **quote screen** has all the instruments on it that you need and that the ones that are trading overnight are flashing for you – particularly the nearby contract you are trading.
4.	Make sure your **television** is working and is set correctly for CNBC and you are getting a good picture. Also, that the remote control is working properly and the level of sound is as it should be, when you press the mute button.
5.	Check that the **telephone** is okay, that the speed dial buttons to the broker are functioning as they should. That the back-up mobile is in an equal state of readiness, with battery charged.
6.	Ensure that you have had your own '**comfort break**' in all respects, so that you are relaxed in every way. Put the 'Do Not Disturb' card or light on the door and then settle down . . .

When the tasks listed above are completed, we are ready to do our preliminary work, to set the scene for Today. First of all, why charts seem to move around on their own, when the computer is switched off, I will never know – but that is my excuse for when the charts are out of place on my screen. But the first thing must be to ensure that you have all the charts you want, laid out in the way you want them – with whatever 'hidden' ones you want to get at having just the smallest part of the edge showing, so that you can click on it fast when needed.

It would be impossible to put things in a definitive order, but over the page are the main tasks I feel are vital to do before the open.

Before the open

1.	Check the overnight action and mark up the 5 min chart with a small line of different colours for the high and low. (I know, there is not a chart in the book with one done, because it would confuse even more, with all the lines that have to be there).
2.	Mark up your daily chart with all the highs and lows and Pivot points within a reasonable area of where the market is likely to move i.e. the current average range.
3.	Transfer the lines to the 5 minute chart, Then double check.
4.	Bring up the Events Calendar (see Figure 10.1) and see what is going on Today. Do a double check with a second calendar if possible. Keep it to hand and if need be mark the relevant times on the chart with an arrow or figure.
5.	Treble check that Alan Greenspan is not pontificating somewhere. It could be a very nasty shock for you, if you do not know about the time that he is speaking.
6.	Then start doing your 'what iffing' concerning the open – particularly if there is a 7.30 Report. Work out exactly what you propose to do if the market bounces, breaks through, whatever.
7.	Look left, by tightening the scale on your screen and see if there is any nearby res/sup that could affect the few bars after the open. Note where the previous congestion is. Check the current trend, the last trend of Yesterday.
8.	Now check what the Spoo is doing overnight. Check the FTSE, which has probably gone into a decline waiting for the bonds to open. If not, why?
9.	Check the 13 min, 34 min, 55 min, 400min/Daily. See how they are stacking up. Where are they in respect of the res/sup lines and what sort of trend have they set up.

Chart 10.1 – Calendar of events
Note: times shown on the E-Signal calendar are EST.

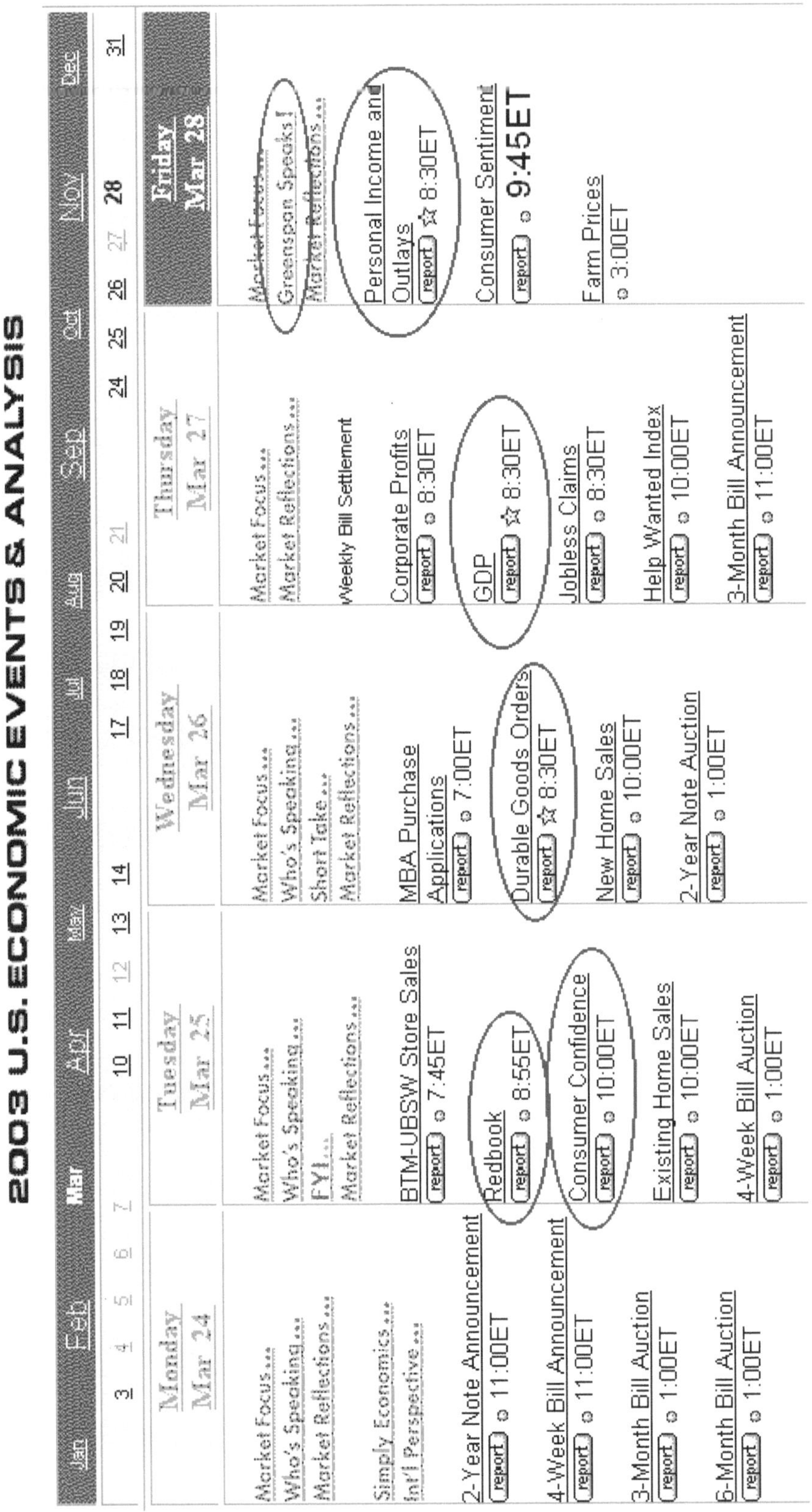

2003 U.S. ECONOMIC EVENTS & ANALYSIS

Jan	Feb	Mar	Apr	May	Jun	Jul	Aug	Sep	Oct	Nov	Dec
3	4 5 6 7		10 11 12 13	14	17 18 19	20 21	24 25	26 27	28		31

Monday Mar 24

Market Focus...
Who's Speaking...
Market Reflections...

Simply Economics...
Int'l Perspective...

2-Year Note Announcement
[report] ⊙ 11:00ET

4-Week Bill Announcement
[report] ⊙ 11:00ET

3-Month Bill Auction
[report] ⊙ 1:00ET

6-Month Bill Auction
[report] ⊙ 1:00ET

Tuesday Mar 25

Market Focus...
Who's Speaking...
FYI...
Market Reflections...

BTM-UBSW Store Sales
[report] ⊙ 7:45ET

Redbook
[report] ⊙ 8:55ET

Consumer Confidence
[report] ⊙ 10:00ET

Existing Home Sales
[report] ⊙ 10:00ET

4-Week Bill Auction
[report] ⊙ 1:00ET

Wednesday Mar 26

Market Focus...
Who's Speaking...
Short Take...
Market Reflections...

MBA Purchase
Applications
[report] ⊙ 7:00ET

Durable Goods Orders
[report] ☆ 8:30ET

New Home Sales
[report] ⊙ 10:00ET

2-Year Note Auction
[report] ⊙ 1:00ET

Thursday Mar 27

Market Focus...
Market Reflections...

Weekly Bill Settlement

Corporate Profits
[report] ⊙ 8:30ET

GDP
[report] ☆ 8:30ET

Jobless Claims
[report] ⊙ 8:30ET

Help Wanted Index
[report] ⊙ 10:00ET

3-Month Bill Announcement
[report] ⊙ 11:00ET

Friday Mar 28

Market Focus...
Greenspan Speaks !
Market Reflections...

Personal Income and
Outlays
[report] ☆ 8:30ET

Consumer Sentiment
[report] ⊙ 9:45ET

Farm Prices
⊙ 3:00ET

The Opening

The first thing you have to check is if the market has gapped; then by how much? You then have to say if it is one to Close, Follow or Either/Way. Take a day like the one shown in Chart 10.2 opposite.

The Big Boys cannot make money when the market is in congestion. Two days running is bad news. Something has to break to give 'em a break! The market… A nice big gap opening is just the job. But it then crept down into a sort of range between the two highs of the previous two days, but it didn't take long for the beginnings of a wedge to form. Then a very good slope pointing the way, followed by the set-up for a TTT – *and* a little Tell-Tale Gap, to give the feeling that a really decent move was in the offing.

With all the build of theses clues, you had plenty of time to seize the opportunity. Because it did indeed come to pass! Complete with a very bullish retracement and a really good run up for the return of the Big Boys. In fact, there was even a return Thank You trade, for all those who can see a decent wedge coming, when it comes. Look again at what sort of homework you had to do. See how much time there was to prepare and get yourself ahead of the game. That is the beauty of the bonds, they may not have a flashy wiggle when they walk, but the measured tread does give you time to weigh things up and come to a reasoned conclusion.

Chart 10.2 – Opening gaps

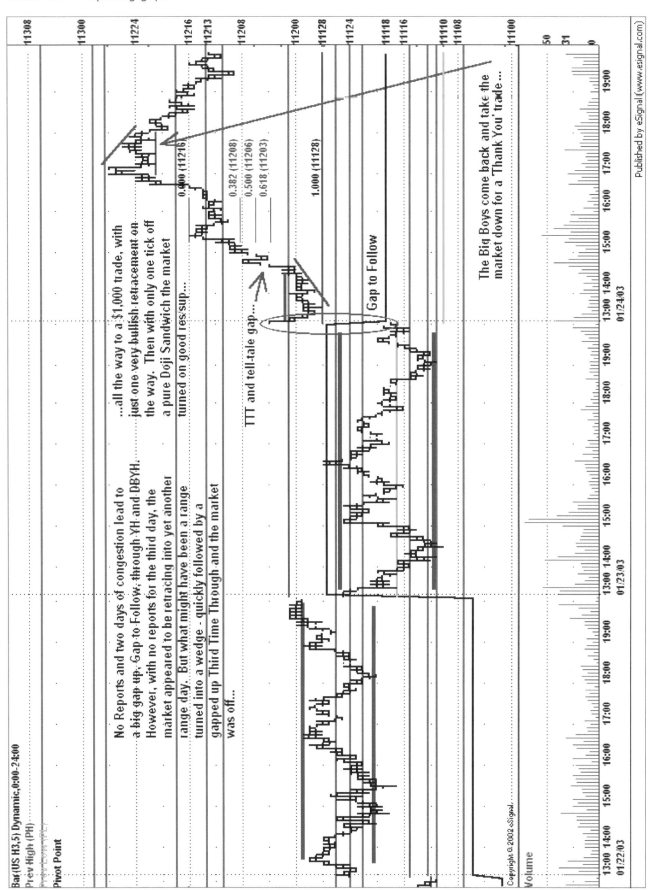

No Reports and two days of congestion lead to a big gap up. Gap to Follow, through YH and DBYH. However, with no reports for the third day, the market appeared to be retracing into yet another range day. But what might have been a range turned into a wedge - quickly followed by a gapped up Third Time Through and the market was off...

...all the way to a $1,000 trade, with just one very bullish retracement on the way. Then with only one tick off a pure Doji Sandwich the market turned on good res/sup...

TTT and tell-tale gap...

Gap to Follow

The Big Boys come back and take the market down for a 'Thank You' trade...

0.000 (11216)
0.382 (11208)
0.500 (11206)
0.618 (11203)
1.000 (11128)

Bar (US H3,5) Dynamic,0:00-24:00
Prev High (PH)
Prev Low (PL)
Pivot Point

Volume

Published by eSignal (www.esignal.com)

Get It Confirmed

And the reasoned conclusion comes from getting the 5 min price action confirmed. Once you get the hang of it, you will find that it becomes second nature to glance at your secondary charts as soon as you have taken your eyes off the 5 min one. You just have to practice all this until you start to get it *off PAT*! Quite deliberately, I have not shown a lot of the 13, 34, and 55 minute charts, because when you are trying just to absorb the concept of price action trading, it can become, or at any rate appear to be, complicated. But just look at the next two charts and you will see how the confirmation from these charts will give you a great deal of confidence to pull the trigger on what you are staring at on the 5 minute chart. Sometimes, they are even ahead. Take a look. You will need to study both these charts carefully.

Chart 10.3 shows quite clearly how, while trading the 5 minute chart, you have really good confirmation of what is going on with the 13 and 34 minute charts. The way the bars build. How on the 5 min you have a J-Hook, which then translates into a deep Downthrust on the 13 min. This allows you to get in early, rather than having to wait and be sure. It helps enormously to be able to work out the r/r/r against a conservative target, with a good chance of being able to achieve a safe stop. You have no way of knowing that it is going to turn into a really big move, but all the time the momentum is building, you are with it.

When the market broke through YH and then the intraday high, which was also the current CH, it would be natural for anyone to get the collie-wobbles when they saw the upthrusting Doji Sandwich, as well as a little (but often very significant) wedge forming. But it didn't cross the line and both the confirming charts did not look as if they want to turn, at all. Not shown on the chart, but the Fib tool, which you would have immediately put up, would also have given you a reading of 'very bullish'. Furthermore, with experience, you will come to realize that most times when the market breaks a significant line in the sand (like the intraday/CH line) it may retrace, but it is going to go on in that direction.

Once it moved away from YH, you would have been able to move your stop up and then the lovely little Tell-Tale Gap would have had you settling back to watch the Ride of the Valkyries into the heavens above. Prudence would have had you out, or certainly taking profits, at the first stall, when the Big Boys came back – but since it was not a reversal pattern, you might well have held on to see just how far it was going.

Chart 10.3 – Combining the 5 min with 13 and 34 min charts

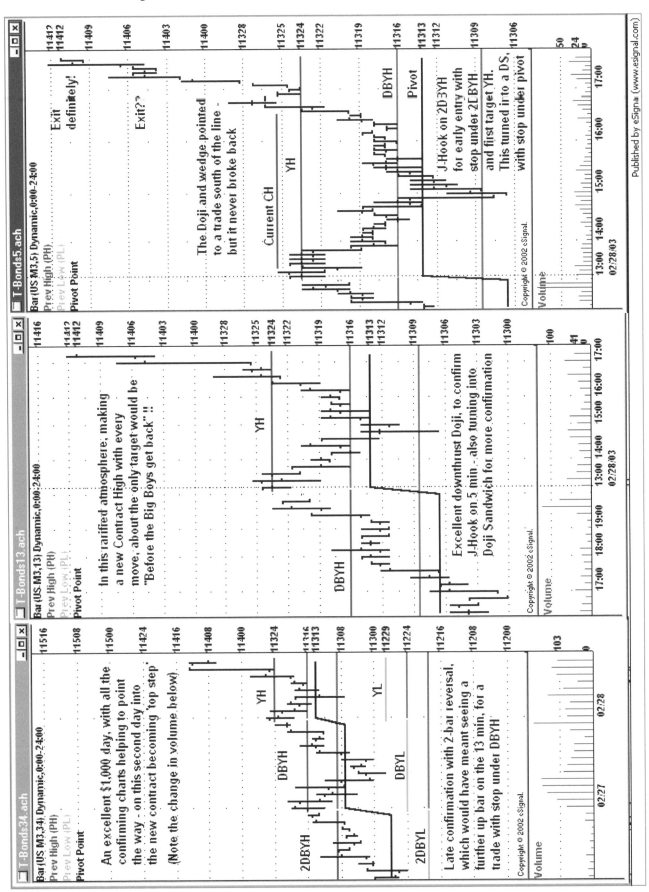

As you can see on Chart 10.4 opposite, the Double Top on what was the new CH heralded what might have been purely a Thank You trade. In the event, the reversal spot on the .382 retracement produced yet another trade, to even higher highs!

Chart 10.4

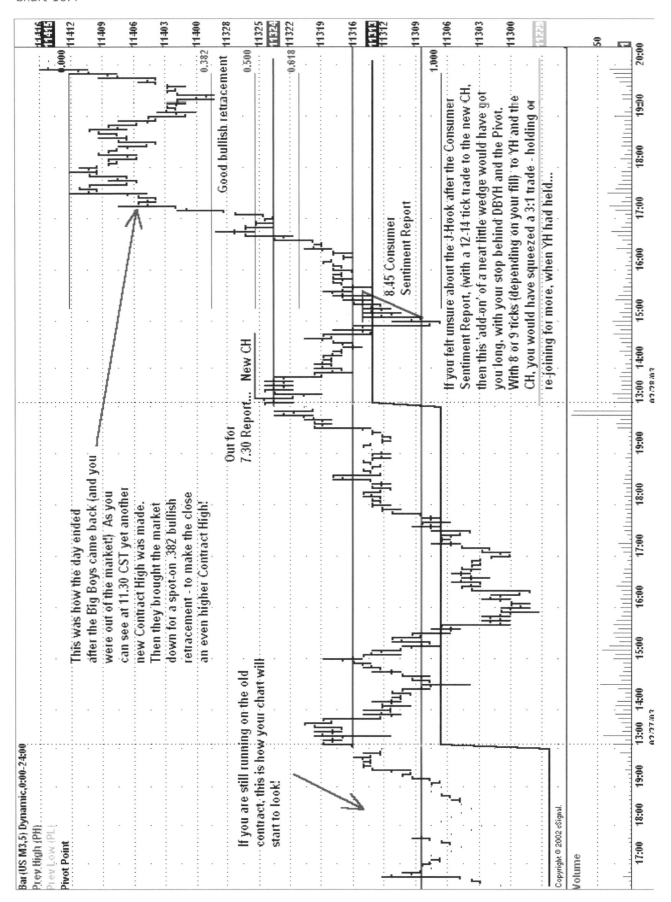

This was how the day ended after the Big Boys came back (and you were out of the market!) As you can see at 11.30 CST yet another new Contract High was made. Then they brought the market down for a spot-on .382 bullish retracement - to make the close an even higher Contract High!

Good bullish retracement

Out for 7.30 Report...   New CH

8.45 Consumer Sentiment Report

If you felt unsure about the J-Hook after the Consumer Sentiment Report, (with a 12-14 tick trade to the new CH, then this 'add-on' of a neat little wedge would have got you long, with your stop behind DBYH and the Pivot. With 8 or 9 ticks (depending on your fill) 'to 'YH and the CH, you would have squeezed a 3:1 trade - holding on re-joining for more, when YH had held...

If you are still running on the old contract, this is how your chart will start to look!

Bar (US M3,5) Dynamic, 0:00-24:00
Prev High (PH)
Prev Low (PL)
Pivot Point

Copyright © 2002 eSignal.

Volume

Look Left, Look Left and Look Left again!

There is just so much to gain from Looking Left. It is staggering how history likes to repeat itself and such a shame that as a generality man is so stupid at learning his lesson of the fact. The examples of how life and often lives could have benefited or been saved if only people had had a regard for history. War, peace, love, you name it – if people had had the sense to Look Left at history, think how many things would have turned out differently. Well, here is certainly a fact which you can gain from, every single day when you settle down in front of your computer to trade. Just Look Left and study and then profit by your endeavours.

In fact, look at the next two charts and you will see as fine an example as you will ever see of having all the information in your hands *before* you trade, in order to profit.

In Chart 10.5 opposite you will see on the Daily that the market plunged down from its CH and then retraced almost exactly to the .382 bearish line, before again setting its sails south. But it appeared to come to an abrupt halt with a Doji – quite a large Doji – right next to a big down bar. Now what does that *look* as if it might do next?

Before you answer, look at the 34 minute chart and take in the fact that the day before had started with a huge Gap to Follow, thundered down the mountain with indecent haste and then close very much on its lows. The Doji bar shot up at 7.30 (I wonder why!) and then went rapidly down from the Wedge to stop just one tick from YL It then went back a full .618 retracement (which means?) – quite so – and then the day ended as a Doji.

Forget for a moment what an excellent trading day that was and ponder on what Tomorrow might bring. We have the possibility of the market making a DS, or even a TTT or, logically, a possible Failed TT. It could also make a Double Bottom, could it not?

Chart 10.5 – Looking left 1

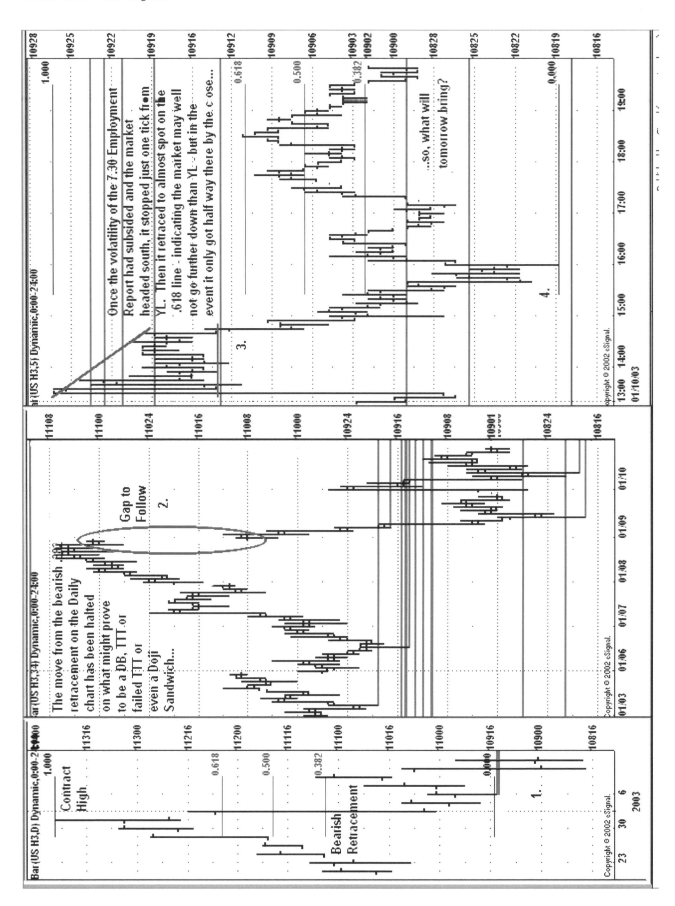

So, armed with all this foresight and having marked your charts up with all the latest data *from looking left* you are all poised for the market to open. With the various 'what-iffing' scenarios we have been through, it is not very surprising to see a large gap (actually, one to Follow), which in fact went below YL and for about a minute gave notice of an Oops trade (I jest, of course!). It then went smartly off to close the gap and head north. With YL and DBYL to hide your stop behind, it would not take much to join the fray in a hurry, with two or three targets on the way, possibly, to YH.

If you had failed to get in and grab a dozen or more ticks, there was even an opportunity to get in on a dead cert .382 retracement – for another dozen. Whatever money there was to be made on the trade, the point is that there was so much information available to get you set on the right path – simply by *Looking Left*. It really is not a question of hindsight. All the information was there to be garnered and evaluated for what it was. We know the market is not always too obliging, which is why we have to take trades with at least a 3:1 ratio, because you are going to lose when it decides to do something else.

This particular trade could have gone wrong after the first couple of bars and shot through the resistance to continue its downward spiral from the CH. If it had, you would have lost a few ticks in the scramble, but such would have been the power of a TTT, in such circumstances, that you would probably have made as much money going the other way. It very often happens that way with a TTT

Chart 10.6 – Looking left 2

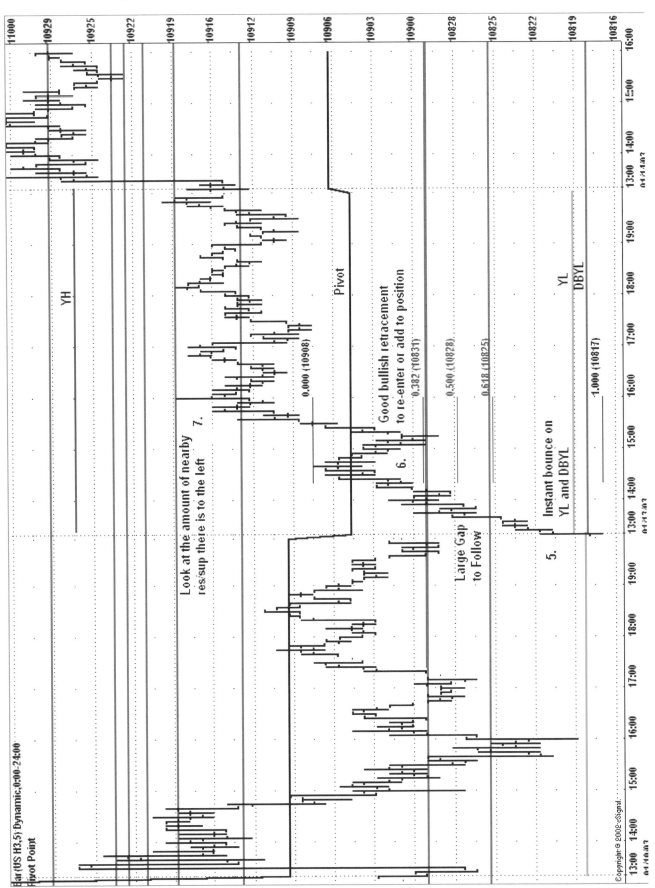

The Man of Pisa

I have often wondered what the modern technical analyst would do if he did not have Fibonacci numbers. Just what set of numbers could he come up with that would do the same job? The mind boggles – particularly if you are, like me, not in the least mathematically minded! I suppose if the truth were known, the reason they work is because they appear so often in nature, in the universe, in the things around us. The numbers just 'go with the flow' and since the market is made up of a seething mass of humanity, they fit into the scheme of things quite naturally.

Anyway, they work like a treat and surely it cannot be long before the Man of Pisa will be part of the school curriculum.

The fact is that the market seems to be glued to those numbers. Just look at Charts 10.6 and 10.7 and see for the umpteenth time how reliable and predictive these retracements are.

Chart 10.7 – Fibonacci retracements

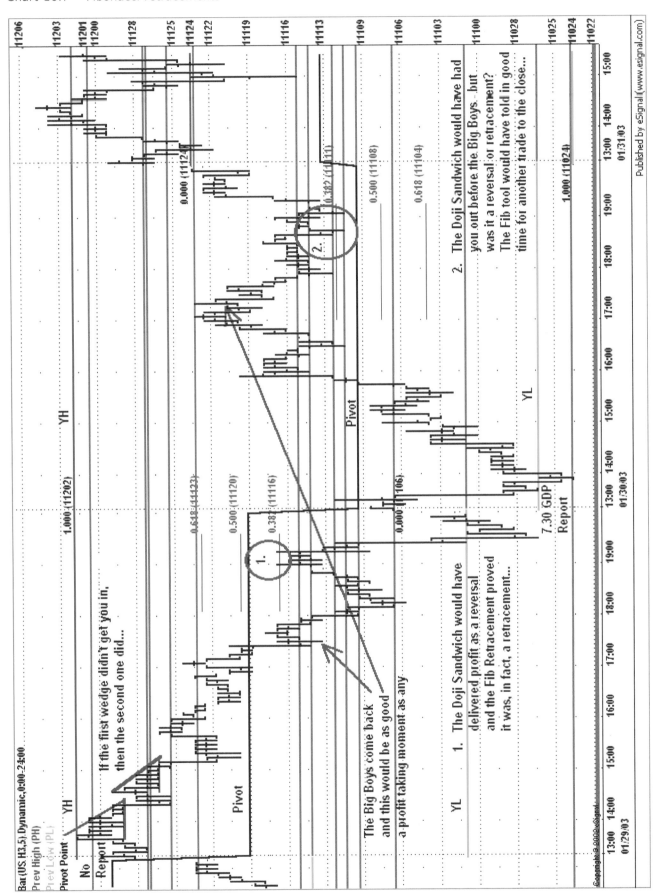

Chart 10.8 – Fibonacci retracements

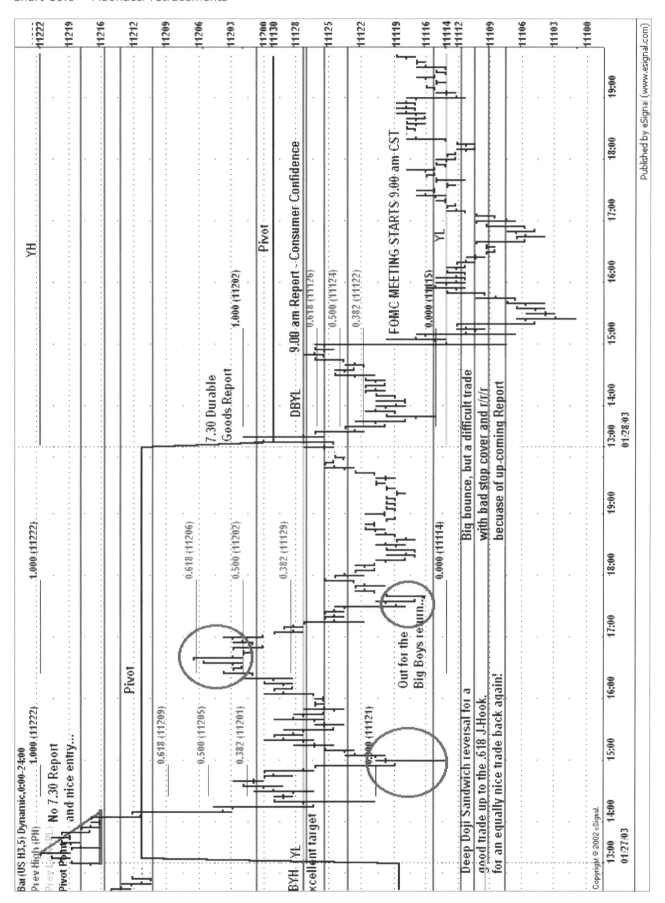

Published by eSignal (www.esignal.com)

By the way, I have never come across anyone else who constantly measures intraday retracements from *only* the high or the low of Today, as it progress. Most seem to find all manner of other points to do the measuring from, but as far as I am concerned, the moving intraday lines are the only reliable places to use. Bearing in mind that the final high and low of Today becomes YH and YL – and just how vital those res/sup lines are – I suppose they are *the* critical points as Today unfolds and the market seems to react to them.

You just have to remember, every time without fail, as soon as you see the market coming off, to put up the Fibonacci tool. If you couldn't get into the market for the reversal, you may well have another chance on the retracement or the Picking Up Stragglers point. If you are in the trade, you immediately have a short term target for when you must call it a day or go the other way. And when the retracement line is directly on a major res/sup line, you have a real banker.

The Fibonacci tool very much helps to concentrate the mind. While on these charts, there are times when it might look a bit confusing having them up, but of course you are only going to have them one at a time (here I have had to have several sometimes on one chart to make a point for you). Just remember this:

1. Markets move up and down most of the time and the first thing one has to find out is whether a reverse move is actually a retracement or a reversal. You need to find out as soon as possible.

2. You have to assess the strength of the pattern you are looking at against the other factors related to Today's price action.

3. You need to consider if the potential of the reversal is a money making opportunity in line with your established risk/reward strategy.

4. If the reversal is a retracement what action should be taken to take profits, add, cover, or stay on the sidelines. A lot of people call a retracement a counter trend trade, but much depends on what time frame you are looking at. It is all a matter of judgment and a constant reassessment of that judgment, in line with the actual price action.

The way the market moves may, in my opinion, best be summed up from that wonderful verse written by the 12th century mathematician Omar Khayyam, in his *Rubáiyát* :

> *The Moving Finger writes, and, having writ,*
> *Moves on; nor all your Piety nor Wit*
> *Shall lure it back to cancel half a Line,*
> *Nor all your Tears wash out a Word of it.*

The Man from the Fed

It really is amazing how long Alan Greenspan has been The Man. He seems to me to be an institution all on his own. It is not what the Fed says, it is what Mr Greenspan says that counts. The markets react very strongly when he is speaking. Obviously when he is addressing a Senate Committee or some other Congressional body, you can expect the markets to hang on his every word. Very often they are totally range bound until he speaks or until the text of his speech is issued and then all hell is let loose! And you need to be out of the market, that's the point. Out on the sidelines.

On other occasions he may be having a lunch or addressing some university and you would think that that would hardly affect the markets. Wrong. While what he says may have little actual affect on the market, if the Big Boys want a reason to move the market, it is just that sort of occasion that provides a beautiful opportunity. Often, for no good reason really, the market can shoot up and then come back down equally fast – just because Alan Greenspan is speaking. A cynic would say that it was just a really good stop-taking manoeuvre, but I couldn't possibly comment...

When The Man is talking, the rule is KEEP OUT.

The Big Boys

Bearing in mind the huge power they exert on the markets and, therefore, on your efforts as a trader, it would seem only fitting to end with the importance of the Big Boys. Whether only a fraction of what is said about them is true or not, it is a fact that their influence is absolute. I have always said that the only way of looking at what they do – or appear to do – is to consider that *they* think it is a huge game. "Taking money from the public," that is what one of their fraternity told me. And it rings in the ears – especially as you and I are members of the public. They can't be beaten, as a collective whole, even if individually they may come and go. When one of the Big Boys enters the pit, you can see all the hands drop, waiting to see what he is going to. When he raises his hands, will they face inwards or outwards – will he be buying or selling? It is fascinating to see it happen.

In fact, let me end by saying that perhaps one of the best bits of advice you will get from these pages is the knowledge that the Big Boys return to the pits at 11.30 CST and that, like the locals in the pits, you should let your hands fall and wait and see what they intend to do. Chart after chart will show you that the market 'does something' at around 11.30 in Chicago. And now you know why - *the return of the Big Boys*!

A Short Post Script

Such is the detail of the subject – Price Action Trading – that you have been studying here, I did not want to dilute the text by going into the many different types of orders and the various forms of execution that are available. I wouldn't go as far as to say that it would take a whole book to cover the subject – but it jolly nearly might! All of it is pretty standard stuff and there is nothing special so far as the T-Bonds are concerned. In any case, much of what you do in that area will depend on the level of trader you are, where you are trading from and what your trading account is like.

Suffice it to say that the real novice can certainly put his toe in the water with spread betting and, indeed, some rather more serious traders (perhaps with not the financial means they would like) might also prefer to trade in this manner. Nevertheless, the experienced trader is going to be using a broker and those who start to trade in multiples of contracts, are going to want a really professional order entry system at the most economic cost around. Only to help put you on the right track, I have detailed in Appendix II what I believe is the latest (and maybe even the greatest!) direct order system into the pits. You can 'test drive' the system on a trial basis; just doing that will, if nothing else, open your eyes to the possibilities of an electronic age which must be approaching its zenith.

Appendix 1

Press release from US Treasury

Concerning the suspension of 30-year bond issuance

EXTRACT FROM THE OFFICE OF PUBLIC AFFAIRS

FOR IMMEDIATE RELEASE
October 31, 2001
PO-749

UNDER SECRETARY OF THE TREASURY FOR DOMESTIC FINANCE
PETER R. FISHER
REMARKS AT THE NOVEMBER 2001 QUARTERLY REFUNDING

Suspension of Thirty-Year Borrowing

The debt management strategy of the Treasury has been to strive to be regular and predictable in the issuance of debt while minimizing borrowing costs over many years and interest rate cycles. The Treasury does not try to outsmart the market at any one moment or to be a "market timer" with respect to any particular shape of the yield curve. However, debt management necessarily involves judgments about the size and duration of the federal government's borrowing needs. This compels us to focus on likely borrowing needs over the coming years but we also take into account the likely consequences of unlikely outcomes.

We do not need the 30-year bond to meet the government's current financing needs, nor those that we expect to face in coming years. Looking beyond the next few years, as I already observed, we believe that the likely outcome is that the federal government's fiscal position will improve after the temporary setback that we are now experiencing.

There are two less likely outcomes that we have also considered.

First, it is possible that the federal government will return to significant and sustained budget surpluses even more quickly than we now expect. In this event, maintaining current issuance levels of 30-year bonds would be unnecessary and expensive to taxpayers.

Second, we face the possibility that sustained surpluses do not materialize as promptly as we now expect. If later in this decade it turns out that 30-year borrowing is necessary to meet the government's financing needs, it is still likely that our decision to suspend 30-year borrowing at this time will have saved the taxpayers money. In addition, the reintroduction of the 30-year bond, at some point in the future, if necessary, would likely be costless to the Treasury.

The 30-year bond no longer maintains a position of significance in the financial markets. Its role and its liquidity have been significantly impaired by the substantial reduction of issuance that has occurred over the last decade. But the markets have functioned smoothly during this period while both activity and attention have shifted to our 10-year offerings.

As long as we have borrowing requirements to finance, the Treasury will seek to maintain the liquidity and depth of the instruments we issue as a means of achieving the lowest cost of borrowing for the taxpayer over time. At this time, the best means for us to do this is to suspend issuance of the 30-year bond and concentrate our borrowing needs on our other instruments.

Appendix 2

Electronic trading in the USA

When you have got up to speed with price action trading you will, eventually, perhaps want to trade multiple contracts in a serious manner. This will mean your wanting the fastest, most accurate quote service available, combined with a professional execution and order entry system that is like trading on-line into the pits – all at a price that makes economic sense.

There are a number of firms to choose from, but here is an excellent one in the shape of Cunningham Commodities Inc. which has been a Clearing FCM and Member Firm of the Chicago Board of Trade since 1982. The firm provides clearing operations for professional floor traders at the CBOT and now provides electronic access through Cunningham Futures Clearing.

The company has built a state of the art electronic network for futures trading, called *Crossfire*, that is capable of providing instantaneous, reliable, and worldwide access for futures traders. Through their network, traders may interact with the electronic markets of the Chicago Board of Trade, EUREX, and Chicago Mercantile Exchange on one screen. As a clearing firm, they give you direct connectivity to the exchanges' electronic platforms. You see on your screen:

- Live Bids and Offers with Volume and last price traded
- Depth of Market
- One click trading and one click cancels
- Net positions
- Audit log of working, filled, cancelled, and stop orders

This is not the old "on-line" order entry system you may be using. This is the latest technology for electronic trading that gives you the same edge on trades as any other trading professional. This software is what their professional traders are using. If you trade electronically, and you don't see live bids and offers on your execution screen, you can now! This flexible electronic trading system delivers a quick and secure platform and here are some of the main features:

- Access to multiple global exchanges including CME, CBOT, and EUREX
- Global 24/7 support
- One Click Trading
- Web browser access
- VPN and T1 access
- Paper Trading (live market - real time)
- Risk and limit management

Fees and Commissions per round turn are, naturally, dependent on the exchange and the volume traded per year. For trading the T-Bonds you could expect to pay a nominal monthly fee and very competitive flat round-turn commission. Clearly *Crossfire* is designed for the serious trader, who is trading multiple contracts, but if you want to see just what it offers you can try the whole thing out, on a trial basis. This is because Cunninghams provides a trading simulator that is a real time application, in that it behaves exactly like the live trading system used by their professional traders. It allows you to trade against the live market depth but with no financial risk. The simulator shows the market depth, volume of each bid and offer, last price traded, and order book. It also has the QuickTrade window which allows you to enter and pull orders rapidly with a single click.

For further information you should contact either:

Cunningham Commodities, Inc.
Chicago
Illinois 6060
Tel: 001 313 939 8950

A&A Trading, Inc,
Chicago,
Illinois 60606
Tel: 800 453 1617

Appendix 3

Glossary of abbreviations and terms

This glossary of terms is based on that produced by the Commodity Futures Trading Commission and I am grateful for their permission to use this abridged version, in which I have also included other terms which I have used within the manual, as well as yet others which you may find useful .

Chart abbreviations

These are the abbreviations which are used throughout the charts:

DBYH	Day Before Yesterday's High*
DBYL	Day Before Yesterday's Low*
CH	Contract High
DS	Doji Sandwich
FOMC	Federal Open Market Committee
JH	J-Hook
YH	Yesterday's High
YL	Yesterday's Low

*When a number precedes the abbreviation it indicates the number of days before
e.g. 2DBYH or 4DBYL

Terms

Accumulate
Buying by traders who are building up a position over time. Referred to in any time frame.

At-the-Market
An order to buy or sell a futures contract at whatever price is obtainable when the order reaches the trading floor. Also called a *Market Order.*

Basis
The difference between the spot or cash price of a commodity and the price of the nearest futures contract for the same or a related commodity. Basis is usually computed in relation to the futures contract next to expire and may reflect different time periods, product forms, qualities, or locations.

Bear
One who expects a decline in prices. The opposite of a bull. A news item is considered bearish if it is expected to result in lower prices.

Bear Market

A market in which prices are declining.

Bid

An offer to buy a specific quantity of a commodity at a stated price.

Bid/Ask Spread

The difference between the bid and ask price. In many markets this spread can be several ticks and in very volatile conditions can open up to unacceptable levels. The FTSE, for example, often has a spread of 4-6 ticks and this can double when the market makes a sudden move. The T-Bonds, however, usually have only has a spread of a tick and it takes exceptional conditions for the spread to open up. At the times when most orders are expected to be placed, it is not unusual to pay the price that is on the screen.

Big Boys .

A term given to major market makers and big players in the pits. While they are always present at the opening and the close, after around 10.30-10.45 CST they drift away for their breakfast or brunch. However, at 11.30 CST – almost on the dot – they collectively seem to return. It is at this time that the market often makes a move, a reversal or shows confirmation of the current trend. It is a time to be wary.

Broker

A person paid a fee or commission for executing buy or sell orders for a customer. In commodity futures trading, the term may refer to:
i) Floor Broker – a person who actually executes orders on the trading floor of an exchange;
ii) Account Executive, Associated Person, registered Commodity Representative or Customer's Man – the person who deals with customers in the offices of futures commission merchants; or
iii) the Futures Commission Merchant.

Bull

One who expects a rise in prices. The opposite of *bear*. A news item is considered bullish if it portends higher prices.

Bull Market

A market in which prices are rising.

Buy (or Sell) On Close

To buy (or sell) at the end of the trading session within the *closing price range*.

Buy (or Sell) On Opening

To buy (or sell) at the beginning of a trading session within the *open price range*.

Cash Price

The price in the marketplace for actual cash or spot commodities to be delivered via customary market channels.

CFTC

See *Commodity Futures Trading Commission.*

Charting

The use of graphs and charts in the technical analysis of futures markets to plot trends of price movements, average movements of price, volume of trading and open interest.
See *Technical Analysis.*

Chartist

Technical trader who reacts to signals derived from graphs of price movements. Western chartist as opposed to Japanese chartist who uses *Candlestick* charting methodology.

Chicago Board of Trade (CBOT)

The premier commodity exchange, best known for housing much of the world's futures trading in agricultural commodities. It is the home of the *30-Year Treasury Bonds.*

Circuit Breakers

A system of trading halts and price limits on equities and derivative markets designed to provide a cooling-off period during large, intraday market movements.

Clearing House

An adjunct to, or division of, a commodity exchange through which transactions executed on the floor of the exchange are settled. Also charged with assuring the proper conduct of the exchange's delivery procedures and the adequate financing of the trading.

Clearing Member

A member of the Clearing House or Association. All trades of a non-clearing member must be registered and eventually settled through a clearing member.

Close

The period at the end of the trading session, officially designated by the exchange, during which all transactions are considered made 'at the close.'

Closing Price (or Range)

The price (or price range) recorded during trading that takes place in the final moments of a day's activity that is officially designated as the 'close.'

CNBC

The prime television channel from the USA that covers all aspects of trading. Based in New York, its programmes are beamed across the world. As soon as news breaks, CNBC is among the first to broadcast it to the world. The 7.00am CST 'Squawk Box' programme, hosted by Mark Haines, is a must for all traders of the T-Bond Futures from Chicago. Anyone day-trading the T-Bonds simply has to have this channel on during trading hours – mute maybe, but ready to turn up for news flashes!

Commission

The charge made by a commission house for buying and selling commodities.

Commodity Futures Trading Commission (CFTC)

The US Federal regulatory agency established by the CFTC Act of 1974 to administer the Commodity Exchange Act.

Commodity Trading Advisor (CTA)

Individuals or firms that, for fees, issue analyses or reports concerning commodities, including the advisability of trading in commodity futures or options.

Congestion

i) A market situation in which shorts attempting to cover their positions are unable to find an adequate supply of contracts provided by longs willing to liquidate or by new sellers willing to enter the market, except at sharply higher prices;
ii) in technical analysis, a period of time characterised by repetitious and limited price fluctuations.

Contract

i) A term of reference describing a unit of trading for a commodity future or option;
ii) An agreement to buy or sell a specified commodity, detailing the amount and grade of the product and the date on which the contract will mature and become deliverable.

Contract High (Low)

The High (Low) of the current contract, it becomes a very key res/sup line in the market. Such points are often marked by a major pattern, such as a *Doji Sandwich, J-Hook* or *Upthrust.*

Contract Month
See *Delivery Month.*

Counter-Trend Trading
In technical analysis, the method by which a trader takes a position contrary to the current market direction in anticipation of a change in that direction.

Cover
i) Purchasing futures to offset a short position. Same as *Short Covering*. See *Offset, Liquidation.*
ii) To have in hand the physical commodity when a short futures or leverage sale is made, or to acquire the commodity that might be deliverable on a short sale.

CTA
See *Commodity Trading Advisor.*

Current Delivery Month
The futures contract which matures and becomes deliverable during the present month. Also called *Spot Month.*

Daily Price Limits
See *Limit (Up or Down).*

Day Before Yesterday's High (Low)
Abbreviated to DBYH or DBYL, they are the next important res/sup lines after Yesterday's High (Low) and are marked on all the charts in this book, as such. For days that precede them the abbreviation has a number placed in front it e.g. 1DBYH, 2DBYH

Day Order
An order that expires automatically at the end of each day's trading session.

Day Traders
Commodity traders, generally members of the exchange on the trading floor, who take positions in commodities and then offset them prior to the close of trading on the same trading day.

Day Trading
Establishing and offsetting the same futures market position within one day.

DBYH
See *Day Before Yesterday's High*

DBYL
See *Day Before Yesterday's High(Low)*

Deck
The orders for purchase or sale of futures and option contracts held by a floor broker.

Default
Failure to perform on a futures contract as required by exchange rules, such as failure to meet a *margin call*, or to make or take delivery.

Delivery
The tender and receipt of the actual commodity, the cash value of the commodity, or of a delivery instrument covering the commodity (e.g., warehouse receipts or shipping certificates), used to settle a futures contract

Delivery, Current
Deliveries being made during a present month. Sometimes current delivery is used as a synonym for nearby delivery.

Delivery Date

The date on which the commodity or instrument of delivery must be delivered to fulfill the terms of a contract.

Delivery Month

The specified month within which a futures contract matures and can be settled by delivery.

Deposit

The initial outlay required by a broker of a client to open a futures position, returnable upon liquidation of that position.

Derivative

A financial instrument, traded on or off an exchange, the price of which is directly dependent upon (i.e. 'derived from') the value of underlying securities, equity indices, debt instruments, commodities, other derivative instruments, or any agreed upon pricing index or arrangement (e.g. the movement over time of the Consumer Price Index or freight rates). Derivatives involve the trading of rights or obligations based on the underlying product, but do not directly transfer property. They are used to hedge risk or to exchange a floating rate of return for fixed rate of return.

Doji Sandwich

The name coined by Bill Eykyn for a specific three-bar reversal pattern, which can be seen in any time frame. It consists of a classic doji bar being sandwiched on both sides by substantial up and down bars (in an up market) and the opposite for a down market. Best seen at good res/sup lines after the market has made a reasonable move.

Downthrust

A large Doji bar with an elongated tail (or head for an *Upthrust*) which signifies that the market can no longer find any interest in prices below (or above) and is about to reverse. Often seen just after *Reports* when the market is very volatile and cynics will say that it is a stop-taking move on the part of the *Big Boys*, before the charge off in the opposite direction.

Elliott Wave

i) A theory named after Ralph Elliott, who contended that the stock market tends to move in discernible and predictable patterns reflecting the basic harmony of nature;
ii) in technical analysis, a charting method based on the belief that all prices act as wavers, rising and falling rhythmically.

Equity

The residual dollar value of a futures, option, or leverage trading account, assuming it was liquidated at current prices.

Failed Third Time Through

See *Third Time Through (TTT)*.

Fast Market

Transactions in the pit take place in such volume and with such rapidity that price reporters are behind with price quotations, so insert 'FAST' and show a range of prices.

FIA

See *Futures Industry Association*.

Fibonacci, Leonardo of Pisa

A thirteenth century mathematician who lived in the city at around the time the Leaning Tower of Pisa was built. He discovered a mathematical series beginning with 1, 1, and where each subsequent number is the sum of the previous two. The series goes to infinity and if each number is divided by the preceding number the result is a constant 1.618. It is from this formula that the Golden Mean stems and the significant ratios of .618, .382 and .500 are introduced as relevant retracement ratios for trading.

Fibonacci Tool

Most good charting package include a means of measuring retracements and extensions. These tools usually have a number of different settings which can be selected for measuring varying distances between any two points on the chart. It is Bill Eykyn's concept to measure retracement from either the intraday high or low, according to which way the market is moving. With market going up, for example a .382 retracement is very bullish, .500 is also bullish, but .618 is unlikely to move much above where the market came off. If the current bar closes below .618, the move is considered to have broken down.

Fictitious Trading

Wash trading, bucketing, cross trading, or other schemes which give the appearance of trading. Actually, no bona fide, competitive trade has occurred.

Fill or Kill Order

An order which demands immediate execution or cancellation.

Financial Calendar

A calendar which informs you of the various financial reports which are due out, as well as the dates of the main meetings at which the Fed Chairman, Alan Greenspan is scheduled to speak.

Financial Instruments

As used by the CFTC, this term generally refers to any futures or option contract that is not based on an agricultural commodity or a natural resource. It includes currencies, securities, mortgages, commercial paper, and indices of various kinds.

Floor Broker

Any person who, in any pit, ring, post or other place provided by a contract market for the meeting of persons similarly engaged, executes for another person any orders for the purchase or sale of any commodity for future delivery.

Floor Trader

An exchange member who executes his own trades by being personally present in the pit for futures trading. See *Local.*

Forced Liquidation

The situation in which a customer's account is liquidated (open positions are offset) by the brokerage firm holding the account, usually after notification that the account is undercapitalized *(margin calls).*

Force Majeure

A clause in a supply contract which permits either party not to fulfil the contractual commitments due to events beyond their control. These events may range from strikes to export delays in producing countries.

Foreign Exchange

Foreign Currency. On the foreign exchange market, foreign currency is bought and sold for immediate or future delivery.

Free Crowd System

A system of trading, common to most U.S. commodity exchanges, where all floor members may bid and offer simultaneously either for their own accounts or for the accounts of customers, and transactions may take place simultaneously at different places in the trading ring. Also see *Board Broker System* and *Specialist System.*

Futures

See *Futures Contract.*

Futures Commission Merchant (FCM)

Individuals, associations, partnerships, corporations and trusts that solicit or accept orders for the purchase or sale of any commodity for future delivery on or subject to the rules of any contract market and that accept payment from or extend credit to those whose orders are accepted.

Futures Contract

An agreement to purchase or sell a commodity for delivery in the future:
- at a price that is determined at initiation of the contract
- which obligates each party to the contract to fulfil the contract at the specified price
- which is used to assume or shift price risk, and
- which may be satisfied by delivery or offset.

Futures Industry Association (FIA)

A membership organization for futures commission merchants (FCMs) which, among other activities, offers education courses on the futures markets, disburses information and lobbies on behalf of its members.

Futures Price

i) Commonly held to mean the price of a commodity for future delivery that is traded on a futures exchange.
ii) The price of any futures contract.

Gaps

At the opening of Today, if the market gaps up or down, the size of the gap can be significant. A gap of up to 8 ticks or an average swing trade is likely to be closed. One of 10/12 plus ticks is probably indicating direction and it is, indeed, a Gap to Follow. One that is in the region of 8/10 ticks should be considered as an Either Way Gap and it is necessary to watch the price action closely.

Give Up

A contract executed by one broker for the client of another broker that the client orders to be turned over to the second broker. The broker accepting the order from the customer collects a wire toll from the carrying broker for the use of the facilities. Often used to consolidate many small orders or to disperse large ones.

Good This Week Order (GTW)

Order which is valid only for the week in which it is placed.

Good 'Til Cancelled Order (GTC)

Order which is valid at any time during market hours until executed or cancelled. See *Open Order*.

Indicators

An indicator is a mathematical calculation that can be applied to an instruments price and/or volume fields, resulting in a value that is used to anticipate future changes in price. Because the current price is a prime element in the calculation most indicators are lagging rather than leading and so more suitable for position rather than day trading.

Inside Day

An Inside Day is defined as having a range which is within the high and low of the previous day.

Inside Day Trade

The rule here is to buy a break on *Yesterday's High* or sell a break on *Yesterday's Low*. While such trades are prone to false breakouts, very often the way the price action sets up and the proximity of significant *res/sup* lines usually helps with the decision making process.

Intraday High (Low)

The high or low made by the market during the day. Unless a range day, usually only one of the intraday line gets taken out as the day starts to trend. It is a key *res/sup* line – made stronger if it has occurred at another previous line, particularly *YH* or *YL*.

Introducing Broker (or IB)

Any person (other than a person registered as an 'associated person' of a futures commission merchant) who is engaged in soliciting or in accepting orders for the purchase or sale of any commodity for future delivery on an exchange who does not accept any money, securities, or property to margin, guarantee, or secure any trades or contracts that result therefrom.

J-Hook

A term introduced to Bill Eykyn by Ken Churchill (now retired from trading), who used to run an excellent service based on *Fibonacci* Spirals. He observed that a big up or down bar which was immediately followed by a reversal bar, which had gapped up (or down) was a particularly strong reversing pattern. Best seen at key *res/sup* lines or deep into new territory.

Key Reversal

A trading event in which price peaks or plummets as a result of buying by squeezed shorts offsetting their positions or squeezed longs selling out in the face of losses. These desperate acts of buying or selling generates unusually high volume, after which the market then moves in the opposite direction.

Large Traders

A large trader is one who holds or controls a position in any one future or in any one option expiration series of a commodity on any one contract market equalling or exceeding the exchange or CFTC-specified reporting level.

Last Trading Day

Day on which trading ceases for the maturing (current) delivery month.

Limit (Up or Down)

The maximum price advance or decline from the previous day's settlement price permitted during one trading session, as fixed by the rules of an exchange. See *Daily Price Limits*.

Limit Move

A price that has advanced or declined the permissible limit during one trading session, as fixed by the rules of a contract market.

Limit Only

The definite price stated by a customer to a broker restricting the execution of an order to buy for not more than, or to sell for not less than, the stated price.

Limit Order

An order in which the customer specifies a price limit or other condition, such as time of an order, as contrasted with a market order which implies that the order should be filled as soon as possible.

Limit Moves

Nearly all markets set *Limits* on the amount of movement that is allowed before trading is halted. With the 30-year Treasury Bonds the limit is 3 points. Whilst not unheard of, it is an exceptional event for the bonds to reach limit. The biggest range days are rarely much over 2 points, while 1 point or $1,000 days occur quite regularly.

Liquidation

The closing out of a long position. The term is sometimes used to denote closing out a short position, but this is more often referred to as covering. See *Cover*.

Liquid Market

A market in which selling and buying can be accomplished with minimal price change.

Local

A member of a U.S. exchange who trades for his own account and/or fills orders for customers and whose activities provide market liquidity. See *Floor Trader.*

Long

i) One who has bought a futures contract to establish a market position;
ii) a market position which obligates the holder to take delivery;
iii) one who owns an inventory of commodities.
See *Short*.

Looking Left

Used throughout this book to signify the act of looking at the previous days, weeks or months of data in order to see where the highs and lows are in order to mark res/sup lines. It is essential to carry out a Looking Left exercise before the start of trading, as part of the important preparation work to set the scene for *Today*. Looking Left is a constant act during the trading day. Many an error can be attributed to a failure to keep assessing the situation by Looking Left.

Margin

The amount of money or collateral deposited by a customer with his broker, by a broker with a clearing member, or by a clearing member with the clearinghouse, for the purpose of insuring the broker or clearinghouse against loss on open futures contracts. The margin is not partial payment on a purchase.
i) Initial margin is the total amount of margin per contract required by the broker when a futures position is opened;
ii) Maintenance margin is a sum which must be maintained on deposit at all times. If the equity in a customer's account drops to, or under, the level because of adverse price movement, the broker must issue a margin call to restore the customer's equity. See *Variation Margin.*

Margin Call

i) A request from a brokerage firm to a customer to bring margin deposits up to initial levels;
ii) a request by the clearinghouse to a clearing member to make a deposit of original margin, or a daily or intra-day variation payment, because of adverse price movement, based on positions carried by the clearing member.

Market Correction

In technical analysis, a small reversal in prices following a significant trending period.

Market-if-Touched (MIT) Order

An order that becomes a market order when a particular price is reached. A sell MIT is placed above the market; a buy MIT is placed below the market. Also referred to as a *board order.*

Market Maker

A professional securities dealer who has an obligation to buy when there is an excess of sell orders and to sell when there is an excess of buy orders. By maintaining an offering price sufficiently higher than their buying price, these firms are compensated for the risk involved in allowing their inventory of securities to act as a buffer against temporary order imbalances. In the commodities industry, this term is sometimes loosely used to refer to a floor trader or local who, in speculating for his own account, provides a market for commercial users of the market.

Market-on-Close

An order to buy or sell at the end of the trading session at a price within the closing range of prices. See *Stop-Close-Only Order.*

Market-on-Opening

An order to buy or sell at the beginning of the trading session at a price within the opening range of prices.

Market Order

An order to buy or sell a futures contract at whatever price is obtainable at the time it is entered in the ring or pit.
See *At-The-Market.*

Momentum

In technical analysis, the relative change in price over a specific time interval. Often equated with speed or velocity and considered in terms of relative strength.

Money Market

Short-term debt instruments.

National Futures Association (NFA)

A self regulatory organization composed of futures commission merchants, commodity pool operators, commodity trading advisors, introducing brokers, leverage transaction merchants, commodity exchanges, commercial firms, and banks, that is responsible – under CFTC oversight – for certain aspects of the regulation of FCMs, CPOs, IBs, LTMs, and their associated persons, focusing primarily on the qualifications and proficiency, financial condition, retail sales practices, and business conduct of these futures professionals.

Narrow Range Days

These are days when the market is going sideways and ends up with a particularly narrow day i.e. with the high and low of the day separated by perhaps only a dozen or so ticks. These tight congestion days often lead to a breakout of the range the following day and a decent trend as well. An *Inside Day* is very often a Narrow Range Day.

Nearby

The nearest delivery months of a commodity futures market.

Net Position

The difference between the open long contracts and the open short contracts held by a trader in any one commodity.

NFA

National Futures Association.

Offer

An indication of willingness to sell at a given price; opposite of *bid*.

Oops Trade

Coined by Larry Williams, the rule is: "If the market opens below Yesterday's Low and trades back to Yesterday's Low, then buy Yesterday's Low." The concept does not usually work the other way round i.e. selling Yesterday's High.

Opening Price (or Range)

The price (or price range) recorded during the period designated by the exchange as the official opening.

Opening

The period at the beginning of the trading session officially designated by the exchange during which all transactions are considered made 'at the opening'.

Open Interest

The total number of futures contracts long or short in a delivery month or market that has been entered into and not yet liquidated by an offsetting transaction or fulfilled by delivery. Also called *Open Contracts* or *Open Commitments*.

Open Order (or Orders)

An order that remains in force until it is cancelled or until the futures contracts expire. See *Good 'Til Cancelled* and *Good This Week* orders.

Open Outcry

Method of public auction required to make *bids* and *offers* in the trading pits or rings of commodity exchanges.

Original Margin

Term applied to the initial deposit of margin money each clearing member firm is required to make according to clearinghouse rules based upon positions carried, determined separately for customer and proprietary positions; similar in concept to the initial margin or security deposit required of customers by exchange regulations. See *Initial Margin*.

Overbought

A technical opinion that the market price has risen too steeply and too fast in relation to underlying fundamental factors. Rank and file traders who were bullish and long have turned bearish.

Overnight Trade

A trade which is not liquidated on the same trading day in which it was established.

Oversold

A technical opinion that the market price has declined too steeply and too fast in relation to underlying fundamental factors. Rank and file traders who were *bearish* and short have turned *bullish*.

Paper Profit or Loss

The profit or loss that would be realized if open contracts were liquidated as of a certain time or a certain price.

Picking Up Stragglers

A phrase coined by Bill Eykyn meaning that the market, having started to make a move in one direction or the other, is often likely to retrace to near that same level, providing another opportunity to join the move, or add to the position.

Pivot High (Low)

A Pivot High or Low is where the market has made a move – perhaps over several days – and then comes off leaving a pivotal position, which the market must take out to continue the trend. Such highs or lows are usually very significant *res/sup* places in the market.

Pit

A specially constructed arena on the trading floor of some exchanges where trading in a futures contract is conducted. On other exchanges the term 'ring' designates the trading area for a commodity. See *Ring.*

Pit Brokers

See *Floor Broker.*

Pit Pivot System

A set of calculations based on *Yesterday's High, Low and Close*, to produce a median point for *Today's* price action, as well as computing the two levels of resistance and support on either side.

Point

A measure of price change equal to 1/100 of one cent in most futures traded in decimal units. In grains, it is of one cent; in T-bonds, it is one percent of par – each point being worth just over $1,000.
See *Tick.*

Point-and-Figure

A method of charting which uses prices to form patterns of movement without regard to time. It defines a price trend as a continued movement in one direction until a reversal of a predetermined criterion is met.

Point Balance

A statement prepared by futures commission merchants to show profit or loss on all open contracts by computing them to an official closing or settlement price, usually at calendar month end.

Pork Bellies

One of the major cuts of the hog carcass that, when cured, becomes bacon.

Position

An interest in the market, either long or short, in the form of one or more open contracts. Also, 'in position' refers to a commodity located where it can readily be moved to another point or delivered on a futures contract. Commodities not so situated are 'out of position'. For instance, soybeans in Mississippi are out of position for delivery in Chicago, but in position for export shipment from the Gulf.

Position Trader

A commodity trader who either buys or sells contracts and holds them for an extended period of time, as distinguished from the *day trader*, who will normally initiate and offset a futures position within a single trading session.

Price Movement Limit

See *Limit* (Up or Down)

Price Patterns

When markets change direction, go into a *congestion*, break out of a channel or *wedge*, or reacts to *resistance* or *support* lines, it tends to make particular price patterns. Many of these are on a repetitive basis and can give a good indication of the market's next move. The same price patterns occur in all different time frames.

Program Trading

The purchase (or sale) of a large number of stocks contained in or comprising a portfolio. Originally called program trading when index funds and other institutional investors began to embark on large-scale buying or selling campaigns or 'programs' to invest in a manner which replicated a target stock index, the term now also commonly includes computer-aided stock market buying or selling programs, portfolio insurance, and index arbitrage.

Public

In trade parlance, non-professional speculators as distinguished from hedgers and professional speculators or traders.

Pyramiding

The use of profits on existing positions as margin to increase the size of the position, normally in successively smaller increments.

Rally

An upward movement of prices. Same as *Recovery*.

Random Walk

An economic theory that price movements in the commodity futures markets and in the securities markets are completely random in character (i.e. past prices are not a reliable indicator of future prices).

Range

The difference between the high and low price of a commodity during a given period.

Reaction

The downward price movement tendency of a commodity after a price advance.

Recovery

An upward price movement after a decline. Same as *Rally*.

Reporting Level

Sizes of positions set by the exchanges and/or the CFTC at or above which commodity traders or brokers who carry these accounts must make daily reports about the size of the position by commodity, by delivery month, and whether the position is controlled by a commercial or non-commercial trader.

Reports

The regular scheduled reports concerning economic data, interest rates, money supply, et al, are the prime movers of the T-Bonds. The most important ones are announced at 7.30am CST, ten minutes after the market opens, and others are scheduled for 9.00am CST, with less important ones at other times. It is vital that small traders are out of the market at these time, but learn to profit from them after the event. Among some of the Reports to be aware of are:

Consumer Confidence	Consumer Price Index	Consumer Sentiment
Consumer Spending	Durable Goods	Employment Situation (First Friday)
Factory Orders	FOMC Announcement	GDP (Gross Domestic Product)
Leading Indicators	Personal Income	Producers Price Index
Redbook	Retail Sales	Wholesale Trade

Resistance

In technical trading, a price area where new selling will emerge to dampen a continued rise. Also see *Support*.

Res/Sup

An abbreviation used throughout this book for the words *Resistance* and *Support*, with particular reference to the lines drawn on a chart.

Resting Order

An order to buy at a price below or to sell at a price above the prevailing market that is being held by a floor broker. Such orders may either be day orders or open orders.

Retracement

A *reversal* within a major price trend.

Reversal

A change of direction in prices.

Risk/Reward/Ratio (r/r/r)

The relationship between the probability of loss and profit. This ratio is often used as a basis for trade selection or comparison. For many traders the r/r/r should not be less than 3:1 i.e. there should be at least 9 ticks from the entry position to the target, if the stop is 3 ticks away from the entry.

Rounded Top (Bottom)

A reversal pattern made by the market over several rising and then falling highs (the opposite for a falling market), so that it is possible to draw a neat semi-circle around the pattern.

Rules

The principles for governing an exchange. In some exchanges, rules are adopted by a vote of the membership, while regulations can be imposed by the governing board.

Scale Down (or Up)

To purchase or sell a scale down means to buy or sell at regular price intervals in a declining market. To buy or sell on scale up means to buy or sell at regular price intervals as the market advances.

Scalper

A speculator on the trading floor of an exchange who buys and sells rapidly, with small profits or losses, holding his positions for only a short time during a trading session. Typically, a scalper will stand ready to buy at a fraction below the last transaction price and to sell at a fraction above, thus creating market liquidity.

Scalping

The practice of trading in and out of the market on very small price fluctuations. A person who engages in this practice is known as a scalper.

Seller's Market

A condition of the market in which there is a scarcity of goods available and hence sellers can obtain better conditions of sale or higher prices. Also see *Buyer's Market*.

Settlement

The act of fulfilling the delivery requirements of the futures contract.

Settlement or Settling Price

The daily price at which the clearing house clears all trades and settles all accounts between clearing members of each contract month. Settlement prices are used to determine both margin calls and invoice prices for deliveries. The term also refers to a price established by the exchange to even up positions which may not be able to be liquidated in regular trading.

Short

i) The selling side of an open futures contract;

ii) a trader whose net position in the futures market shows an excess of open sales over open purchases. See *Long*.

Short Covering

See *Cover*.

Short Selling

Selling a futures contract with the idea of delivering on it or offsetting it at a later date.

Slippage

Slippage is the number of ticks lost or gained as a result of the market moving after the order has been placed and before it has been filled in the market.

Small Traders

Traders who hold or control positions in futures or options that are below the reporting level specified by the exchange or the CFTC.

Speculator

In commodity futures, an individual who does not hedge, but who trades with the objective of achieving profits through the successful anticipation of price movements.

Spread (or Straddle)

The purchase of one futures delivery month against the sale of another futures delivery month of the same commodity; the purchase of one delivery month of one commodity against the sale of that same delivery month of a different commodity; or the purchase of one commodity in one market against the sale of the commodity in another market, to take advantage of a profit from a change in price relationships. See also *Arbitrage, Switch*. The term spread is also used to refer to the difference between the price of a futures month and the price of another month of the same commodity. A spread can also apply to options.

Stall

When a market is moving sideways in a tight range – usually after having moved in one direction or the other and is about to reverse. Mainly applied to *tick* and one minute charts. See *Stop Taking Tick*.

Stop-Close-Only Order

A stop order which can only be executed, if possible, during the closing period of the market. See also *Market-on-Close Order*.

Stop Limit Order

A stop limit order is an order that goes into force as soon as there is a trade at the specified price. The order, however, can only be filled at the stop limit price or better.

Stop Order

This is an order that becomes a market order when a particular price level is reached. A sell stop is placed below the market, a buy stop is placed above the market. Sometimes referred to as *Stop Loss Order*. Can also be a *Profit Stop*, which is usually instigated against a pre-determined risk/reward ratio of profit, when the trade is entered.

Stop Taking Tick

Seen when the market has stalled and puts in one tick below or above the market, before moving off in the opposite direction, thus catching traders with stops too close to the market. See *Stall*.

Straddle

See *Spread.*

Strong Hands

When used in connection with delivery of commodities on futures contracts, the term usually means that the party receiving the delivery notice probably will take delivery and retain ownership of the commodity; when used in connection with futures positions, the term usually means positions held by trade interests or well-financed speculators.

Support

In technical analysis, a price area where new buying is likely to come in and stem any decline.
Also see *Resistance.*

Taking Out Stops

A phrase referring to the market dipping below a support line (or above resistance) before moving in the opposite direction. It appears as if the *Big Boys*, having made their own decision to take the market in one direction, deliberately put the market in the opposite direction for long enough to Take Out Stops, before then making the move they intended all along.

T-Bond

See *Treasury Bond.*

Technical Analysis

An approach to forecasting commodity or securities prices which examines patterns of price change, rates of change, and changes in volume of trading and open interest, without regard to underlying fundamental market factors.

Tell-Tale Gap

This is a small gap (usually only one tick on a 5 minute chart) that appears as the momentum suddenly occurs in the market. Many times seen as the market moves through strong *res/sup* lines – often giving rise to a good trading opportunity.

Thank You Trade

A name given by Bill Eykyn to an often seen phenomenon after a good trending day, when the market reverses – as if to say 'Thank You' to the *Big Boys* for the ride.

Third Time Through (TTT)

A term used by Bill Eykyn to describe a break out pattern which many times occurs when the market is in a range. It appears to attack the line, once, twice and then goes through on the third occasion. If an elongated range, sometimes the attack may show itself as a pair of reversal bars. Usually, the last few bars before the third attack have lower lows. A Failed TTT is an equally powerful reversal signal – often causing a TTT in the opposite direction.

Tick

Refers to a minimum change in price up or down. In the T-Bonds it is 1/32nd so that there are 32 ticks in one point. When referring to a price in writing, the point is separated by the symbol ^ from the ticks; thus 129^15 is spoken, as in a given order, "One twenty-nine, fifteen". Each tick is worth almost exactly $32, so that there is just over $1,000 in each point.

Today

Today is used throughout this book to describe the current day's price action. When a day's trading starts, it is referred to as Today for the whole of the session. Tomorrow never comes and Yesterday generally has the most impact on Today.

Trader

i) a merchant involved in cash commodities;

ii) a professional speculator who trades for his own account.

Transaction

The entry or liquidation of a trade.

Treasury Bills

Short-term U.S. government obligations, generally issued with 13, 26 or 52-week maturities.

Treasury Bonds (or T-Bond)

Long-term obligations of the U.S. government which pay interest semi-annually until they mature or are called, at which time the principal and the final interest payment is paid to the investor.

Treasury Notes

Same as *Treasury Bonds* except that Treasury Notes are medium-term and not callable.

Trend

The general direction, either upward or downward, in which prices have been moving.

Trendline

In charting, a line drawn across the bottom or top of a price chart indicating the direction or trend of price movement. If up, the trendline is called bullish; if down, it is called bearish.

Upthrust

See *Downthrust*

Unemployment Report

The most important monthly report to affect the T-Bonds, it comes out on the first Friday of every month at 7.30am CST. It is essential to be out of the market when this report is announced. Now often referred to as *Unemployment Situation* or in colloquial speech – 'The Numbers'.

Volume of Trade

The number of contracts traded during a specified period of time. It may be quoted as the number of contracts traded or in the total of physical units, such as bales or bushels, pounds or dozens.

Wash Trading

Entering into, or purporting to enter into, transactions to give the appearance that purchases and sales have been made, without resulting in a change in the trader's market position.

Weak Hands

When used in connection with delivery of commodities on futures contracts, the terms usually means that the party probably does not intend to retain ownership of the commodity; when used in connection with futures positions, the term usually means positions held by small speculators.

Wedges

A common term among technical analysts for a price pattern of higher highs or lower lows which can be large or small when formed into a classic wedge. Unless a pennant, the wedge usually has a flat bottom or top and it is from this side that the market normally breaks out.

Appendix 4

Recommended reading

There is a legion of books you could buy and I have to say that I have collected quite a few over the years. Most now just gather dust on my bookshelves because they are simply not relevant to my method of trading. Some are of interest, but only a very few are of real value, to me. It is not that the books are written by people who do not know their subject (most are acknowledged experts), it is just that the subjects are not relevant to what I now believe to be the way to trade.

For example, I started in the market with index options. Initially, that was through responding to a newspaper advertisement and believing that I had stumbled upon the system of all systems. It was a question of just 'ring up the broker and he will tell you when he gets a 'buy' signal' and you buy. Well, we needn't dwell on the disastrous results, but it made me buy some books on what option trading was all about. Just because I had bought a pup, didn't mean to say money couldn't be made out of options per se. As you can imagine, I bought and now have quite few books on options! I also have a couple of computer programs for options that never get used now, too!

Candlestick charting

I have a couple of books on candlestick charting and I had a computer program for that, too. It was an old DOS system and has now crashed for the last time. Candlesticks are certainly a most interesting way of looking at charts. I am sure there is something in the concept and the patterns can be most interesting. Some of them definitely come up trumps a lot and the names are always fun, but many of the chart patterns are exactly the same as Western charting patterns and it is just a question of a rose by another name.

If you want to find out what it's all about get *Candlestick Charting Explained* by Greg Morris.

Elliot Wave

As I have mentioned, Elliott Wave is a big thing with some traders. For me it is wonderful *after the event* and that's no good! But there are position traders who swear by the concept and there are several computer programs wholly based on EW.

Anyway, if you want to find out about the rudiments get *The Elliott Wave Principle* by Frost and Prechter. If nothing else, you will see just how relevant Mr Fibonacci is. You will appreciate that the waves would probably mean nothing if it wasn't for the fact that all them are based on Fibonacci numbers. It is the fact that they are that makes Elliott Wave worth understanding – well at least the principle of it.

Fibonacci Applications

Now a book that really is worth getting is *Fibonacci Applications and Strategies for Traders* by Robert Fischer. It also covers, incidentally, the logarithmic spiral and how the concept works. Quite deep stuff. The book also goes into some detail on how you can project 'time targets' using the Fibonnaci retracement numbers and combining extensions and corrections, as well as computing 'time goal days'. There really is some good material in this book, but I feel you need to be trading in a longer time frame than one day to make the most of it. That means, for me, a whole different ball game – that could end up with sleepless nights. Not, as they say, my bag, but it could be something you might care to investigate, once you are a seasoned price action day trader!

I have already mention Larry Williams and I am sure you would find: *How I made One Million Dollars Last Year Trading Commodities* a really good read. It is dated, of course, and I only wish I had bought it in 1979, in the sense that I wish I had started trading then. As you might expect, there are masses of books you can get on all the various different aspects of trading. If you want to trade the grains, there are a host of expert books; if you want to trade the precious metals, there is a another bunch of authors from whom you can absorb wisdom and understanding on the subject. There are niche books for niche markets, there are books on trading with the stars and the planets, there are books on buying with the full moon and selling with the new moon – or is it the other way round? Just look at some of the headings you can find in the booksellers' catalogues: fundamental analysis; on-line investing; market timing; short selling; chaos and cutting edge; global investing; discipline and psychology; astro-cycles; emerging markets. The list is endless. There will be pearls in all of them I am sure, but exactly what aid they will be to your making money, I do not know.

'You can't tell till you bet!'

However, the most entertaining and in many ways the most informative book that you must read is *Reminiscences of a Stock Operator* by Edwin Lefevre. It costs less than $20 from all the leading trade booksellers and it is excellent bedside reading. It has some wonderful lines in it, including: "You can't tell till you bet!" Based on the life of legendary trader Jesse Livermore, who at 15 was making a good living out of the stock market, at the turn of the last century. It has to be the classic example of 'reading the tape' – if only because in his day that was all there was to read. The ticker tape. It is certainly the book that made me realize that that was what one had to do now, as then. If you can learn to read the tape, you don't need all the fancy indicators and systems. You don't need to search for this illusory Holy Grail. You don't need to ask other people's opinion on the market. You don't need to play another man's game. You just have to do it!

Global-Investor

Well, that is my extremely short list of recommended reading. You can, however, get a hugely expanded list from the Global-Investor bookshop. In fact, about which here are a few words:

Global-Investor is a mail order and online bookseller specializing in investment and trading books. It stocks a full range of British and American finance books from all the main publishers and many of the smaller ones. Most books are held in stock and can be sent on the day you order. One especially useful service is that Gi prepares free book summaries of all the books it stocks detailing the chapter headings and contents, the jacket text, the author's background and any independent reviews. All this information is available on their website:

http://www.global-investor.com

Gi also publishes a 60-page catalogue of all the books which it sells, which is available free and well worth getting.

Global-Investor
43 Chapel Street
Petersfield
Hampshire
GU32 3DY

Tel +44 (0)1730 233870
Fax +44 (0)1730 233880